Developing a Pitcher

Developing a Pitcher

From Youth to High School

Preston B. Bilhartz
Rocky D. Bilhartz, MD, MBA

2025
GREEN PUBLISHING HOUSE, LLC
Bryan/College Station, Texas

Developing a Pitcher: From Youth to High School

Copyright © 2025 by Green Publishing House, LLC

Full-page photographs in Chapter 3 (p. 12), Chapter 4 (p. 20), Chapter 5 (p. 34), Chapter 6 (p. 44), and Chapter 7 (p. 68) by Eva Dorman

Full-page photograph in Chapter 4 (p. 4) by Lindsey L. Bilhartz

Cover page and design by Preston B. Bilhartz and Rocky D. Bilhartz

All rights reserved. Printed in the United States of America. No part of this book may be reproduced or distributed in any form or by any means, or stored in a database or retrieval system, without the written permission from the publisher, Green Publishing House, LLC, including, but not limited to, in any network or other electronic storage or transmission, or broadcast for distance learning. Some ancillaries, including electronic and print components, may not be available to customers outside of the United States.

ISBN 978-1-63432-042-9 (paperback)
ISBN 978-1-63432-043-6 (PDF)
ISBN 978-1-63432-044-3 (EPUB)

www.GreenPublishingHouse.com

"
Success always favors
the one hustling.
—R. Bilhartz

TABLE OF CONTENTS

CHAPTER 1
Introduction
The Lab at HUSTLE3 2

1

CHAPTER 2
Start with a Routine
Dynamic vs. Static Warm-Ups 6
The Warm-Up 8

5

CHAPTER 3
Learning to Throw
Throwing Mechanics 14
Tee Ball Age 16
Machine Pitch Age 17
Learning to Throw Routine 17

13

CHAPTER 4
Learning to Pitch
Programming Workouts 22
Learning to Pitch Drills 23
Helpful Tips & Caveats
  for Instructing the Drills 31

21

CHAPTER 5

Equipment for Pitchers

Prioritize First 37
Prioritize Secondarily 40
For the Most Dedicated 42

35

CHAPTER 6

Arm Care & Velo Program

Off-Season & Pre-Season 62
In-Season 64
After the Season 66
Rest & Recovery 67

45

CHAPTER 7

Bullpen Pitching

Pitch-Type & Grip 70
Flat-Ground Pitching 75
Bullpen Routine 76
What's the Ideal Age for Curveballs? 79

69

CHAPTER 8

Strength Program

The Early Years: Bodyweight Training 86
The Later Years: Resistance Training 92
The Lifts 94
Accessory Exercises 96

83

CHAPTER 9

Workout Templates

Off-Season Template 102
Pre-Season Template 106
In-Season Template 110
Templates for Younger Youth 114

101

Acknowledgments 117 ■ **About the Authors 119** ■ **Index 121**

1
Introduction

> **"Simplicity is the ultimate sophistication.**
> —Leonardo da Vinci

Pitching is the key to winning baseball games at any level. Hitting and fielding help, but without strong pitching, you'll struggle to make it through the first elimination game of your Little League tournament, and without pitching, you will never win an NCAA championship.

Pitching is a skill deeply rooted in talent, and some players start with more than others. Some throw harder and look more "natural" with their delivery from the very beginning, but talent alone is not enough. In order to be a pitcher, you must learn precise movement patterns and develop the muscle memory needed to consistently throw strikes. The more strikes you can throw, the more opportunities you'll earn—and the more chances you'll have to improve.

The real question is just how to *begin*.

DEVELOPING A PITCHER

In recent decades, the methods used for sports performance training in pitching have evolved alongside the technological advances of our day. More can be captured now on video, and in slower motion. More can be measured: the speed, the spin, the path of the ball, and the ground forces generated from the pitcher. These are all metrics that can be found in modern player assessment portfolios.

Complex approaches to strength training, arm care, and building arm velocity have emerged at pitching facilities across the country. The number of elite-level instructors that offers somewhat competing philosophies for performance training and injury prevention continues to grow. On one hand, the environment for developing pitchers has never been more exciting. On the other hand, it has never been more difficult for engaged parents to navigate with their child.

Knowing where to start can be hard, but creating *simple* and *sustainable* training programs that work for players in the youth to high school years is even harder. That's why we wrote this book.

The Lab at HUSTLE3

HUSTLE3 has been a regional leader in sports performance training since 2020. At the youth level, our training philosophy is embodied in two simple goals that we set for our athletes:

1. **Learn to be a great competitor.**
2. **Learn not to overreact when things don't go your way.**

In order to be a great competitor, you must develop confidence in what you do, and confidence is built through discipline and consistency. That *consistency*, perhaps more so than anything else, is the most difficult trait to find at the youth and high school levels. Kids are highly dependent upon parents and other adults for their transportation, motivation, training resources, and overall encouragement.

While high school upperclassman may be less dependent on adults to get to and from training locations, their competing time commitments—from schoolwork, college preparatory planning, social networks, extracurricular activities, and the sheer volume of games being played during an athletic season—place equal or greater challenges on what can consistently be done.

School sports and strength training programs, by their very nature, must be geared more toward team development, and at times, they will be incomplete and offer inconsistent training for individual players. This means it is essential for athletes—or baseball pitchers—at this level to develop some consistency in their daily routines and take self-ownership of their workouts.

While complex and constantly changing day-to-day routines run by professional trainers throughout the in-season, off-season, pre-season, and post-season, may make sense for the collegiate and professional athlete, we have found this complexity to be counterproductive at times for the majority of youth trying to develop simple muscle memory skills and generalized strength. This is not to say that routines that change week-to-week and differ from season-to-season should not be implemented for certain athletes as they progress in their development. However, we have witnessed that when players at this level are unable to easily memorize their daily routines for arm care, muscle memory, bullpen throwing, strength, conditioning, and flexibility, their program won't get done frequently enough to show consistent progress.

We have achieved the best results from youth to high school when our sports performance programs are *simple* enough to be *sustainable*. In this book, we intend to outline some of the science behind what we do, and show you some of the equipment and technology we specifically incorporate to optimize training efficiency. We will explain the pitching drills, arm care, and strength programs that have worked for our players at the youth and high school levels, so that you can hopefully replicate our success for yourself or your player.

Developing a Pitcher *begins* here, so let's get started.

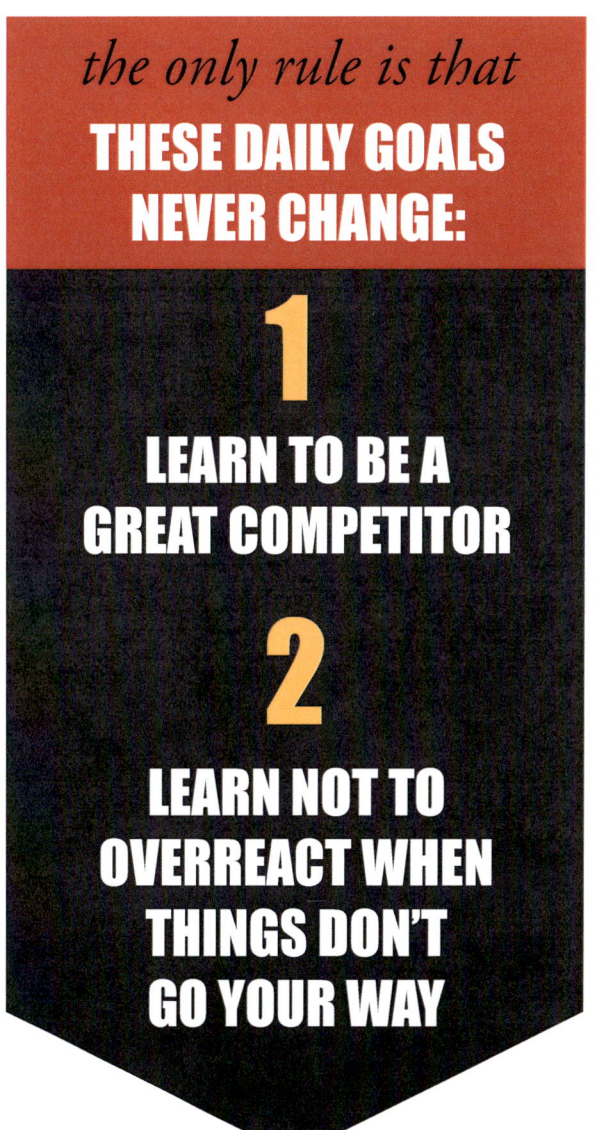

the only rule is that
THESE DAILY GOALS NEVER CHANGE:

1 LEARN TO BE A GREAT COMPETITOR

2 LEARN NOT TO OVERREACT WHEN THINGS DON'T GO YOUR WAY

2
Start with a Routine

> **Successful people do daily what others do occasionally.**
> —Paula White

Whenever you find yourself uncertain or confused as to what you should be doing in life, start with a new routine. At younger ages, when it comes to sports performance training, we ingrain the following concepts into our athletes:

- "I must warm-up."
- "I must workout."
- "I must recover."

This framework will embody the athlete's approach to training for the remainder of his or her athletic career, however long or short that might be. It must be taught at the early ages, so that it will be *routine* at the later stages, when producing maximal effort and preventing injury become the athlete's foremost goals.

Be aware that the time required for an athlete to warm-up and recover will vary by competition level. While it is not uncommon for most of our collegiate and professional athletes to warm-up for more than 30 minutes before their workouts, the time needed to warm up 6-year-old kids is frequently *overestimated* at Tee Ball practice by a well-meaning and energetic coach.

Kids, in general, do not require nearly as long of a warm-up, as they are usually ready to go at the speeds in which they move. Their heart rates normally beat faster at rest than their adult counterparts, and their core body temperatures can be more quickly warmed with brief-duration activities, given their lower body surface areas.

That is not to say that warm-up routines should not be performed at younger ages, or that 30+ minutes of warm-up is always required for more elite players. We are just emphasizing that while the reason for the warm-up remains the same at all levels—to increase flexibility and range of motion while elevating body temperature and blood flow—the scope and duration of warm-up activities will need to be appropriate for age and competition level.

The same is true when it comes to aspects of recovery following individual workouts. You will typically need to recover *less* when you *do less*. For example, there's not a huge need for any recovery following a standard Tee Ball practice, but recovery takes on new meaning when you have just thrown 75 pitches at a velocity of 80+ mph. Remaining cognizant of these simple principles will keep you ahead of most amateur coaches.

Dynamic vs Static Warm-Ups

Although the details are beyond the scope of this book, you should be aware that some controversy has existed within exercise science in recent years about whether athletes should warm up using a dynamic (movement-based) or a static (standard stretching) protocol. Early research[1] suggested

---

1 Fowles, J.R., et al. "Reduced strength after passive stretch of the human plantarflexors." *J Appl Physiol.* 2000;89(3):1179–1188.

the basic routine

Warm-Up → Workout → Recover

Repeat

that static stretching might actually temporarily impair the strength of muscular contractions, so this is what prompted a shift by many toward emphasizing more dynamic warm-up routines that appeared to better enhance muscular power.[2] More recent studies, however, have not shown the same detrimental effects of static stretching before workouts,[3] and both types of routines have been shown to be superior to no warm-up at all.[4]

The main point to convey is that nuances clearly exist regarding the duration of warm-ups performed, the specific activities done, and the athletes studied. That said, both dynamic warm-up and static stretching routines appear to have a role in preparing the body to perform and are incorporated in our approach here.

In the rest of this chapter, we will outline the warm-up routine that we perform with our youth players prior to any throwing, strength, or skill-building activities. The same basic warm-up routine will be carried into the high school years, with some minor modifications and additions that we will discuss more about in later chapters as we get deeper into our pitcher-specific practices and year-round programming.

---

2 Yamaguchi T, and Ishii K. "Effects of static stretching for 30 seconds and dynamic stretching on leg extension power." J Strength Cond Res. 2005;19(31):677–683.

3 Samson M., et al. "Effects of dynamic and static stretching within general and activity specific warm-up protocols." J Sports Sci Med. 2012;11(2):279.

4 Little T., and Williams, A.G. "Effects of differential stretching protocols during warm-ups on high-speed motor capacities in professional soccer players." J Strength Cond Res. 2006;20(1):203–307.

the purpose of the warm-up

1
Increase flexibility and range of motion

2
Elevate body temperature and blood flow

DEVELOPING A PITCHER

The Warm-Up

The following drills are recommended to be performed in sequential order. Actual distances or durations of time recommended may be modified as needed for age and competition level. Dynamic exercises can be performed "in place" and without the need for a large area, if space is limited.

Scan for Video of Full Routine

Dynamic Warm-Up & Static Stretching Routine

HIGH KNEES

Perform at a moderate pace. Jog linearly in the forward direction while bringing each knee above the waist and towards the chest. Pump the arms accordingly.

DISTANCE: 30 feet (ft) in one direction, rest briefly, then 30 ft back.

BOTTOM KICKERS

Perform at a moderate pace. Jog linearly in the forward direction, bending each knee backward so the heel can touch the bottom. The thigh should remain in a vertical position and not lift up toward the chest. Pump the arms accordingly.

DISTANCE: 30 ft in one direction, rest briefly, then 30 ft back.

START WITH A ROUTINE | 2

KNEE HUGGERS

Perform at a **very slow**, deliberate pace. Step with one leg, and then grab the knee of the opposite leg, bringing (or "hugging") it up to the chest. Return the leg to the ground. Alternate legs back and forth, while walking the distance.

DISTANCE: 30 ft in one direction, rest briefly, then 30 ft back.

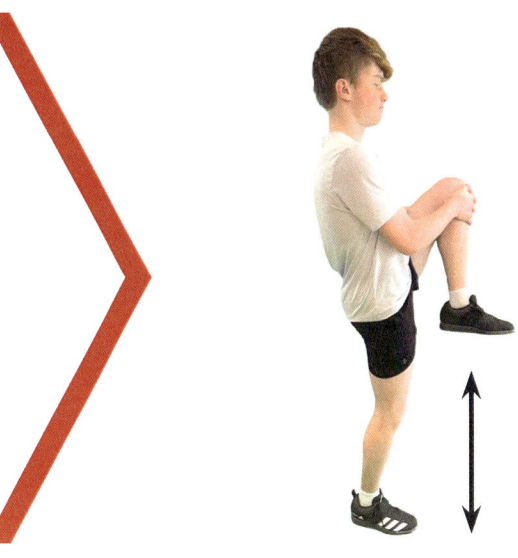

CRADLE WALKS

Perform at a **very slow**, deliberate pace. Step with one leg, and then grab the side of the opposite leg's foot, pulling (or "cradling") it up to the waist. Return the leg to the ground. Alternate legs, back and forth, while walking the distance.

DISTANCE: 30 ft in one direction, rest briefly, then 30 ft back.

LUNGES WITH TWIST

Perform at a **very slow**, deliberate pace. Step with one leg, and bend the front knee, allowing the back knee to almost (but not quite) touch the ground. Hold that position and twist the upper torso from side to side. Alternate legs while walking the distance.

DISTANCE: 30 ft in one direction, rest briefly, then 30 ft back.

DEVELOPING A PITCHER

SIDE LUNGES

Perform slowly. Start with both legs straight and spread apart wide. Shift the body to one side, bending the knee while keeping the opposite leg straight. Shift the body to the other side. Repeat back and forth, trying to get the bottom closer and closer to the heel on the bent leg side.

DURATION: 30 seconds.

GROIN STRETCHES

(A) Start in a deep squat position. Place elbows on the inside of the knees and press outward while the legs provide resistance. (B) Then, place arms on the outside of the legs and pull inward while the legs provide resistance pushing outward.

DURATION: 20 seconds for (A), and 20 seconds for (B).

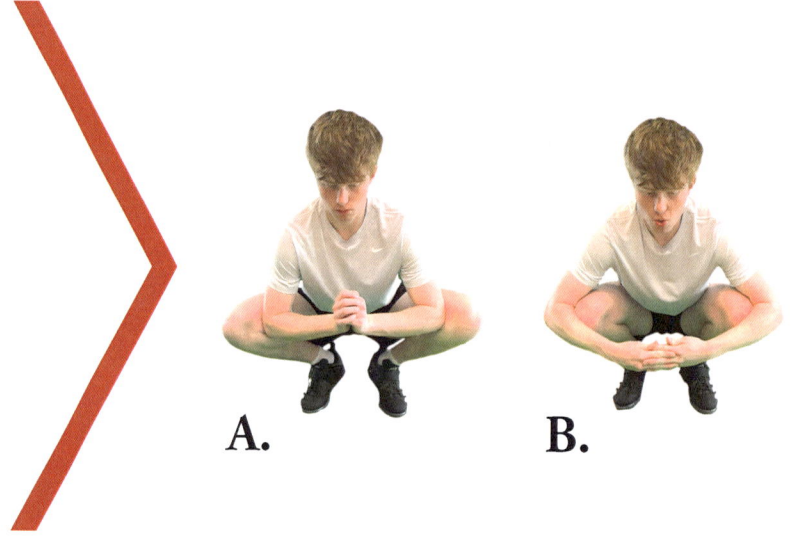

SPIDERS

Perform slowly. (A) Place the right elbow inside a bent right knee and touch the right toe. Hold for the duration. Stand up. (B) Then, place the left elbow inside a bent left knee and touch the left toe. Hold for the duration.

DURATION: 20 seconds for (A), and 20 seconds for (B).

START WITH A ROUTINE | 2

ARM CIRCLES & FLAPS

(A) Start with arms outstretched and rotate shoulders in a forward circular motion. Pause, and rotate them backwards. (B) Then, position arms with elbows bent at 90°, one upright and one downward. Flap arms up and down, reversing their positions.

DURATION: 15 seconds each direction, forwards and backwards, for (A), and 15 seconds for (B).

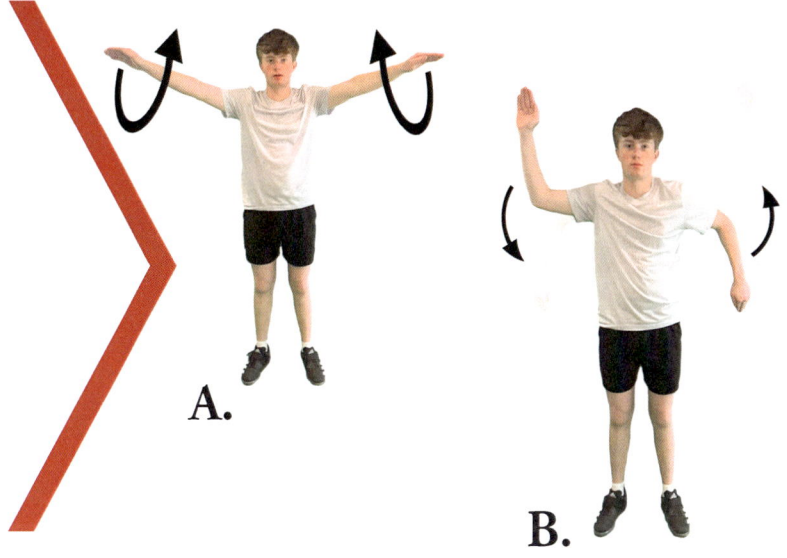

PULL ACROSS & PULL BEHINDS

(A) Pull one arm across the chest and hold for the duration. Repeat with the other arm. (B) Then, bend one arm behind the head and pull the elbow down with the other hand. Hold for the duration. Repeat with the other arm.

DURATION: 15 seconds / arm for (A), and 15 seconds / arm for (B).

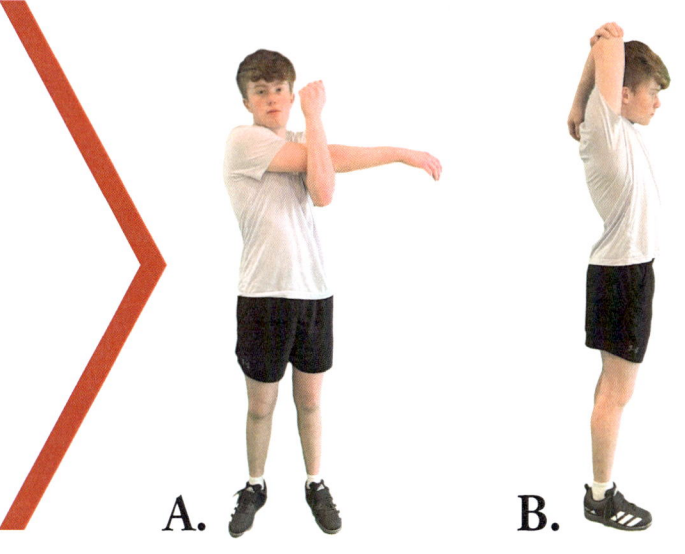

SHOULDER LIFTS

(A) Start with the arms at the sides. Lift each arm out in front, with thumbs up. Return to the sides. (B) Lift each arm out in front 45° from the midline, with thumbs horizontal. Return to the sides. (C) Lift each arm directly outward, with thumbs down. Return to the sides. Cycle (A), (B), and (C).

DURATION: 30 seconds.

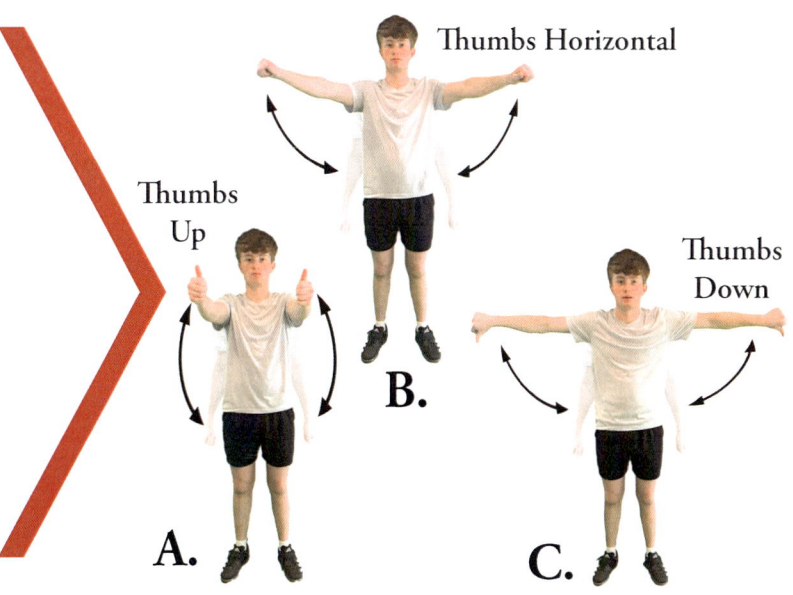

3
Learning to Throw

> "
> The journey of a thousand miles begins with a single step.
> —Lao Tzu

This will not surprise you, but it is worth stating: youth pitchers are less precise than their professional counterparts. We are not referring to them being less accurate, although that is true, too. We are just conveying that youth pitchers have more variability in their body movements from pitch to pitch than those who perform at higher competition levels.[1] Being able to replicate a successful pitching motion over and over again, from the start of the delivery to the release point, is hard to do. High school pitchers can do it better than youth pitchers. College pitchers outperform high schoolers, and Major League

....

1 *Fleisig, G. et al. "Variability in baseball pitching biomechanics among various levels of competition." Sports Biomech. 2009 Mar;8(1):10-21.*

13

DEVELOPING A PITCHER

pitchers outperform Minor Leaguers. At each level of increasing competition, more precision in movement patterns is found. This is a reflection of developing muscle memory.

They say it's easier to learn new motor movement patterns when you are younger. Just ask anyone over the age of 40, who has never been snow skiing, how challenging it is to pick up the skill. The activity requires balance, control of body weight, strength, and muscle memory to navigate the bumps and turns of the mountain slope.

Learning to pitch has its own set of muscle memory challenges, including the adaptations players will need to make from youth to high school as their own anatomy changes and body grows in size and strength. Starting to build baseline throwing and pitching movement patterns at a younger age will work to a player's advantage later on. While there is no specific age cutoff, our experience would say that the activities outlined in this chapter are most effective when done with individuals prior to the age of 10.

Throwing Mechanics

Much gets talked about when it comes to throwing mechanics and for good reason: the pitching arm must generate, and then subsequently withstand, a number of powerful forces with every pitch. At the highest competition levels, peak stress on the pitching elbow can measure over 100 Nm, or the equivalent of holding a 55 lb kettlebell behind your head with your wrist/elbow bent backwards, every pitch. When throwing a baseball, the pitching shoulder rotates about 180

degrees and can reach internal rotational speeds upwards of 9000 degrees per second.[2] In recent years, the "epidemic" of arm injuries has gotten plenty of mention, but perhaps more striking is how the arm, rather miraculously, survives the throwing motion at all.

With the widespread availability of slow-motion video and data analytics at the collegiate and professional levels, our current study of throwing mechanics continues to reach new heights. Is a fastball more effective when thrown from a *wider* or a *more narrow* horizontal release point? What about a curveball? Which pitch puts *less stress* on the arm and elbow?

Of course, being able to collect more data does not necessarily mean we know (yet) how to truly analyze it all and make perfect sense of it. Moreover, a spreadsheet of numbers likely means nothing to Little Johnny who is merely wanting to play catch in the backyard. So, the question remains: how do we best put this all together *simply* for the youth athlete to grasp? Baseball begins for all of us as a kids' game, and it must *still be fun*.

──────────────────────────────

2 *Driveline Baseball.* "The Truth Behind Pitching Mechanics." YouTube, https://www.youtube.com/watch?v=p5D1kmLgPQw. Accessed 3/29/2025.

Keeping this in mind, our approach to throwing mechanics is to recognize that:

- All players are their own unique athletes, each with different anatomical proportions and natural movement tendencies.

- More than one mechanical throwing pattern has proven to be effective in pitching. There is not a single "look" we are striving to reproduce in every player. We value working within a youth athlete's "natural" throwing motion as much as possible.

- Throwing mechanics can largely be improved without specifically focusing on them at all during full-speed throwing activities. Instead, we have our youth players consistently perform a progression of drills, as a part of their warm-up routine, each time that they throw. The drills are geared toward developing the neuromuscular pathways that are necessary for the upper and lower body to interact collectively during the complex motion of throwing.

In the remainder of this chapter, we will outline the *Learning to Throw* drills that we recommend introducing at the younger competition levels, and then in the following chapter, we will explain the addition of a second set of muscle memory routines specific for pitching development.

BUILDING MUSCLE MEMORY

DEVELOPING A PITCHER

Tee Ball Age

Most baseball-playing youth will participate in Tee Ball by ages 5 or 6. It is here that we begin our early instruction in throwing mechanics.

We conceptually divide the space behind the thrower into two halves relative to an imaginary vertical line down the middle of the player's head and back (Figure 3.1). We refer to these different halves as the "Back Side" and the "Throwing Arm Side." Then, we place the player's arm in the "High-Cocked Position" (Figure 3.3), so the player knows the *feel* of the elbow being bent behind the head with a ball in the hand. After this basic instruction, we are ready for the first drill.

Starting with the ball in the throwing hand, we

Figure 3.1

have the player perform 3 progressions:

1. Drive the elbow down and to the "Back Side." (Figure 3.2)
2. Bring the arm up to the "High-Cocked Position." (Figure 3.3)
3. Step and throw, releasing the ball through the "Throwing Arm Side." (Figure 3.4)

Scan for Visual of Throwing Motion

When we work individually with one kid at a time, we perform repetitions with an iPad setup on a tripod behind the player. We use the *Video Delay Instant Replay Pro* app (for iOS); which enables a player to make a throw and then look back at the screen to see their movement replayed. We want players to make sure they are driving their elbow and arm to the "Back Side." We frequently use video analysis in our training at all levels, but we have found this technique to be particularly useful in developing shoulder-hip separation (what occurs when you reach to the "Back Side") in our youngest throwers.

Figure 3.2 Back Side.

Figure 3.3 High-Cocked Position.

Figure 3.4 Throwing Arm Side.

Machine Pitch Age

By ages 7 or 8, most players will be participating in Machine Pitch. At this level, the *Learning to Throw* routine begins to integrate upper and lower body movements together. We perform the following drills in succession several days a week (at individual or team practices). Approximate distances and/or durations of time recommended may be modified as needed for age and competition level.

Scan for Visual of Learning to Throw Routine

GRIP AND ELBOW FLIPS   DURATION: 2 min | DISTANCE: 8-10 ft

EXPLAINED: (A) Standard grip: 2 fingers on top and others tucked underneath. (B) Modified 3-finger grip for most players at this age (until hand grows). (C) With the throwing elbow resting on the glove, flip the elbow forward, and snap the wrist down. Release the ball to your partner.

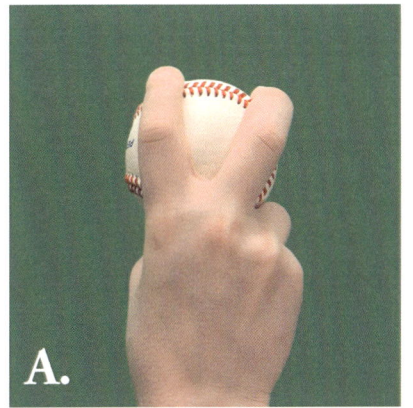 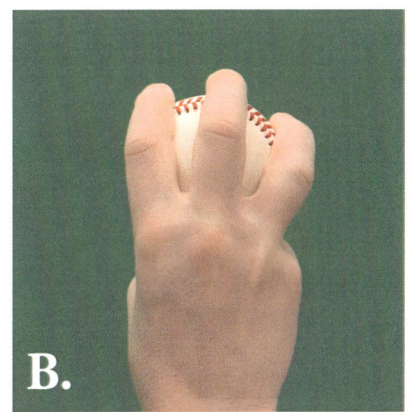 

TWIST AND THROWS   DURATION: 2 min | DISTANCE: 20-30 ft

EXPLAINED: (A) Stand with the side of the throwing shoulder pointing toward your partner. (B) Keeping the feet anchored in the ground, twist the torso ≥ 90° so the chest (and then the glove-side shoulder) face your partner. (C) Reach the arm back and throw the ball to your partner.

DEVELOPING A PITCHER

ROCKERS
DURATION: 2 min | DISTANCE: 50ft

EXPLAINED: (A) Stand with the feet spread apart wide. (B) Rock forward, bending the front knee to get as low as possible. (C) Then, rock backward, bending the back knee. Finally, throw to your partner, pushing off with the back leg while straightening the front knee on the release.

HOP-HOP THROWS
DURATION: 3 min | DISTANCE: 70 ft

EXPLAINED: (A) Begin by slightly lifting the front leg off the ground to stand on the back leg only. (B) Hop forward toward your partner. (C) Then, quickly hop forward again, and throw. Focus on forcefully swinging the front leg up at the start to initiate higher and higher hops.

WHIP BEHINDS

DURATION: 3 min | DISTANCE: 70 ft

EXPLAINED: Stand with the feet spread apart wide. Whip the back leg behind the front leg to spring the body forward in a linear direction, and then throw to your partner. The total distance the back foot moves from the starting point to the landing point (see below) should be approximately two times the width of the player's initial stance.

CLOUD TOUCHES

DURATION: 5 min | DISTANCE: Max

EXPLAINED: Get a 5-10 ft running start and throw to your partner. Prior to release, perform either a "crow hop" (a single large hop like the first part of the *Hop-Hop Throws* drill) or a leg "whip behind" (as done in the *Whip Behinds* drill). As the hands separate to initiate the throw, focus on getting the glove (or glove-side shoulder) pointed upward to the sky ("cloud touches").

4
Learning to Pitch

> **Spectacular achievement is always preceded by unspectacular preparation.**
> —Robert Schuller

Youth players will begin to participate in "kid-pitch" baseball by at least the ages of 9 or 10. The *Learning to Throw* routine will remain ongoing, but *Learning to Pitch* drills will now gain obvious importance. There are many common pitching faults (seen at the later stages) that can mostly be avoided if appropriate muscle memory patterns are ingrained early on.

The *Learning to Pitch* drills outlined in this chapter are designed to foster the development of balance, bodyweight strength, and the coordinated directional movements necessary to become a successful pitcher. We have seen those who perform them routinely gain confidence in themselves as pitchers: "I do drills at practice that pitchers do. Therefore, I am a pitcher."

DEVELOPING A PITCHER

We recommend performing these drills 3 days per week, beginning in the month leading up to every season, and then throughout the season. The drills do not take much time to complete. They can be performed on a typical baseball practice day after the warm-up and throwing routine, and prior to any bullpen pitching. They can also be performed as a stand-alone activity, or integrated into a bodyweight strength training program (discussed more in Chapter 8).

Programming Workouts

The "programming" of weekly workouts (to be outlined in Chapter 9) will be most applicable for players entering the high school years, but it still deserves a brief mention here. First of all, we recognize that youth baseball pitchers will (and should) have natural gaps in their baseball training throughout the year. There will be other sports participation (we encourage this), family vacations and events, recreational camps, and other activities that will compete with a player's weekly routine. **Simple patterns of practice, however, can be instilled at young ages**.

We set the following weekly training goals for our youth pitchers during the baseball season:

- Baseball-specific activities, 2-3 days per week
- Strength/athleticism-building activities, 2-3 days per week
- *Learning to Pitch* drills, which can easily be integrated into either of the above routines, 3 days per week

Baseball-specific activities will most commonly be a team practice or a group/private instructional lesson. These activities will usually be the greatest time commitment for a youth player, typically up to 1-2 hours daily when performed. We incorporate the *Learning to Pitch* drills into many of these baseball specific practices when we oversee them.

simple youth programming...

Baseball-Specific Activities
2-3 days/week

Strength/Athleticism-Building Activities
2-3 days/week

3 days/week
Learning to Pitch **Drills**
(integrated into the above activity days)

Strength/athleticism-building activities, at this age, will require less of a daily time commitment. These activities can even be done at home, completed in under 30-45 minutes daily after a brief warm-up, and the *Learning to Pitch* drills can easily be integrated into them, too.

This means a standard baseball in-season week (if no weekend baseball games are scheduled) would look something like this for a youth player:

> **MONDAY:**
> Strength/athleticism-building activities (with *Learning to Pitch* drills)
>
> **TUESDAY:**
> Baseball (team) practice (with *Dynamic Warm-Up* & *Learning to Throw* routines)
>
> **WEDNESDAY:**
> Strength/athleticism-building activities (with *Learning to Pitch* drills)
>
> **THURSDAY:**
> Baseball (team) practice (with *Dynamic Warm-Up* & *Learning to Throw* routines)
>
> **FRIDAY:** OFF
>
> **SATURDAY:**
> Strength/athleticism-building activities (with *Learning to Pitch* drills)
>
> **SUNDAY:**
> Baseball (individual) practice (with *Dynamic Warm-Up* & *Learning to Throw* routines)

This weekly routine will obviously need modification throughout the season, as the timing of games and other extracurricular activities will ultimately impact the days training can take place. The key is to establish a routine that can be done consistently enough with youth pitchers to start their development of muscle memory.

Learning to Pitch Drills

As we have already discussed, each of the 7 drills outlined on the following pages can be done as a part of either a baseball-specific or strength/athleticism workout. The drills are designed to be performed in sequential order, and completed in their entirety in under 15-20 minutes.

The drills are collectively geared toward developing all the aspects of the pitching delivery and the motor patterns needed, including:

- The initiation of a pitching *rhythm* and the generation of a *high-enough* leg kick;
- The synchronous separation of the hands downward at the same time the lifted-leg begins to drive to the ground;
- The return of both hands (in a "W" motion) back upward, ending with the *glove-side* (front shoulder) being "high to the sky";
- The *tuck of the glove* into the armpit, prior to the release of the ball, and the rotation of the chest over the glove;
- The front plant foot landing *in-line* with the back foot after pushing off from the rubber.

Each of these components will be re-discussed, where applicable, in the individual pitching drills that follow.

DEVELOPING A PITCHER

4-STEP WINDUP & BALANCE DRILL

- 10 Reps (Windup Only)
- 10 Reps (Balance Added)

Why it's a good drill...

Pitchers need to develop a "rhythm" with their movement patterns. The 4-Step Windup trains the shifting of body weight, rhythmically, into a high leg kick. The Balance Drill helps to build strength to lift the leg higher and more easily.

Scan for Video Tutorial of Drill

EXPLAINED: (A) Stand with both feet side by side at a 30-45° angle to the pitching rubber. Take a small step backward (STEP #1) with the front foot. (B) Make a "block step" (STEP #2) with the back foot, squaring it up to the rubber. (C) Lift the front leg high (STEP #3) to the chest. (D) Stride forward, landing the front foot in-line with the back foot (STEP #4). This completes a single repetition, as the entire throwing motion does <u>not</u> need to be completed here. After performing 10 repetitions of the windup only, complete 10 more repetitions, but add in the Balance Drill: Pause at STEP #3 for at least 5 seconds while holding the leg high in the air, before progressing on to STEP #4.

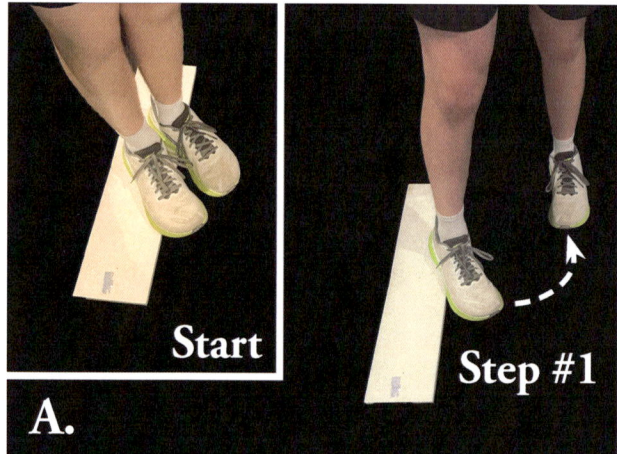

SEPARATION DRILL

- 10 Reps

Why it's a good drill...

Pitchers require synchronous activation of the upper and lower body when driving towards home plate, and this starts with the separation of the hands. If this initial movement is out of sync, everything after that will be difficult to correct. The Separation Drill helps to develop the timing that is needed.

Scan for Video Tutorial of Drill

EXPLAINED: (A) Start with both feet shoulder-width apart and the back foot engaged with the pitching rubber (i.e., the "stretch" position). (B) Lift the front leg high (STEP #3 of the 4-Step Windup) keeping the throwing hand, that is holding the ball, inside the glove. (C) Separate both hands downward at the same time that the front leg starts to drive to the ground, and return both hands back upward in a "W" motion. (D) As the front foot touches the ground, the glove-side (front shoulder) should be pointed "high to the sky," and the throwing arm should be in the "high-cocked" position (as explained in Chapter 3).

A.

B.

C. "W" Motion

D.

DEVELOPING A PITCHER

NOSE OVER TOES DRILL

■ 10 Reps

Why it's a good drill...

Leaning too much in one direction at the start of the pitching motion will lead to pitchers having to overcompensate later on with other movements, and this is a setup for failure. The Nose Over Toes Drill focuses on developing balance and maintaining an upright posture throughout the delivery.

Scan for Video Tutorial of Drill

EXPLAINED: (A) Start with a baseball in the throwing hand, and perform the 4-Step Windup. (B) At STEP #3 of the 4-Step Windup, think about the Separation Drill and begin to separate the hands at the same time the lifted leg drives to the ground. (C) After the front foot plants and completes the final step of the 4-Step Windup, freeze and assess where the upper body is positioned, relative to an imaginary line connecting the toes of the back foot to the toes of the front foot. (D) Avoid leaning too far forward or too far backward. The "nose should be in-line with the toes." If not, correct the body's position, and then repeat the repetition, trying to return exactly to the same (and correct) position, again and again.

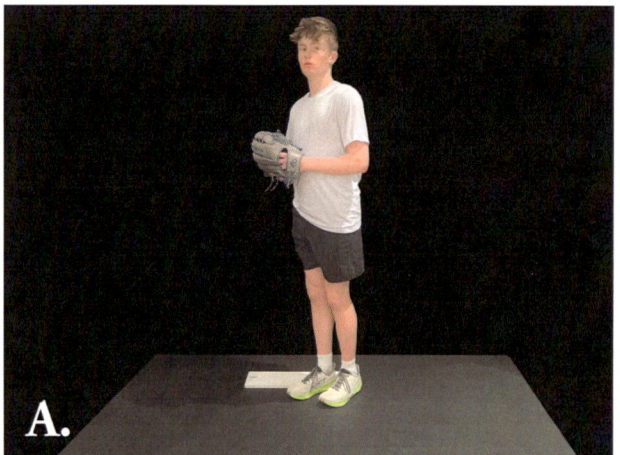
A.

B.

C. *Correct (nose in-line with toes)*

D. *Incorrect (nose too far forward)*

LEARNING TO PITCH | 4

TAPE DOWN THE MOUND DRILL
- 10 Reps

Why it's a good drill...
Learning to step in-line straight down the mound helps the pitchers consistently throw more accurately by avoiding the common faults associated with finishing too open (exposing the release of the ball too soon to the hitter) or too closed (forcing pitchers to throw across their bodies).

Scan for Video Tutorial of Drill

EXPLAINED: (A) Place a piece of tape on the ground (or on a mound), extending out from the pitching rubber, in the direction of home plate. (B) Holding a baseball in the throwing hand, start to perform the 4-Step Windup. (C) At STEP #3 of the 4-Step Windup, think about the Separation Drill and begin to separate the hands at the same time the lifted leg drives to the ground. (D) After the front foot plants, freeze and assess where the front plant foot is located relative to the tape. Avoid landing too far open or too far closed. The plant foot should be directly in-line with the tape. If not, correct the body's position, and then repeat the repetition, trying to land the front foot directly in-line with the tape, again and again.

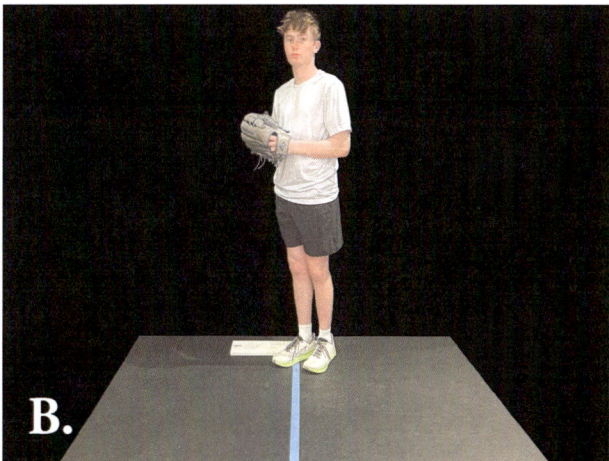

DEVELOPING A PITCHER

CHEST OVER KNEE DRILL

- 10 Reps

Why it's a good drill...

Finishing with a "flat back" can be an unnatural movement pattern for youth pitchers. The Chest Over Knee Drill helps to train this finish while building strength and balance in the front leg. Focus on "glove-side high" at the start, then tuck the glove into the armpit and end with a flat back.

Scan for Video Tutorial of Drill

> **EXPLAINED:** (A) Holding the middle of a wrapped towel in the throwing hand, place the back push-off leg on a chair. (B) Position the "glove-side high" with the front shoulder pointing up. (C) Pull the glove to the chest and down into the armpit, extending the throwing arm out to reach a maximum distance. (D) Finish with as flat of a back as possible. Return to the starting position and complete the next repetition. If the front leg tires before all repetitions are complete, pause to rest for a moment, and then finish. The more the drill is done, the stronger the front leg will become, and the easier it will get to complete all repetitions without pausing.

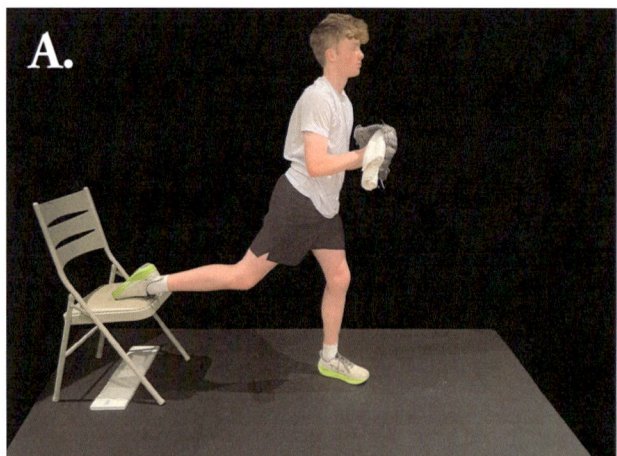

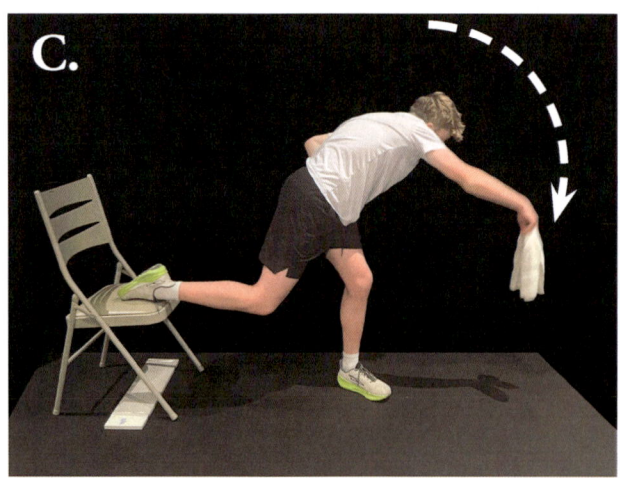

LEARNING TO PITCH | 4

GLOVE-SIDE TUCK DRILL

- 10 Reps

Why it's a good drill...

The Glove-Side Tuck Drill helps youth pitchers to not "open up" their chest too soon and pull the ball across their body. By tucking the glove and not flying open, the pitcher's center of gravity remains more mid-line, aiding pitch accuracy, and hiding the ball longer from the view of the hitter.

Scan for Video Tutorial of Drill

> **EXPLAINED:** (A) Holding the middle of a wrapped towel in the throwing hand, start by performing the 4-Step Windup. (B) At STEP #3 of the 4-Step Windup, think about the Separation Drill and begin to separate the hands into a "glove-side high" position at the same time the lifted leg drives to the ground. (C) As the body drives forward, pull the glove into the chest and down into the armpit. (D) Complete the throwing motion with as flat of a back as possible. Think about the chest "rolling over" the tucked glove to finish.

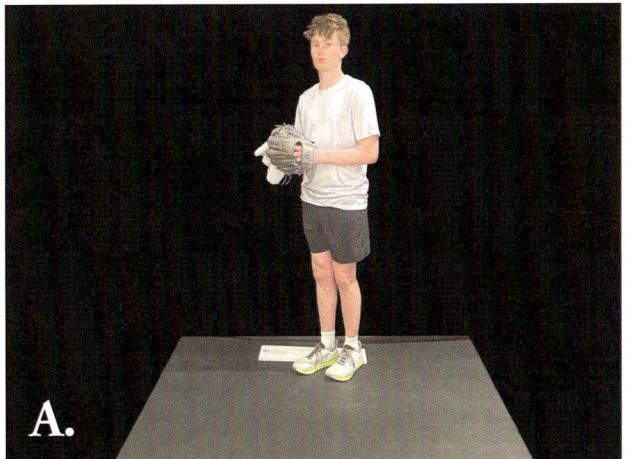

A.

B.

Tuck the glove into the armpit

C.

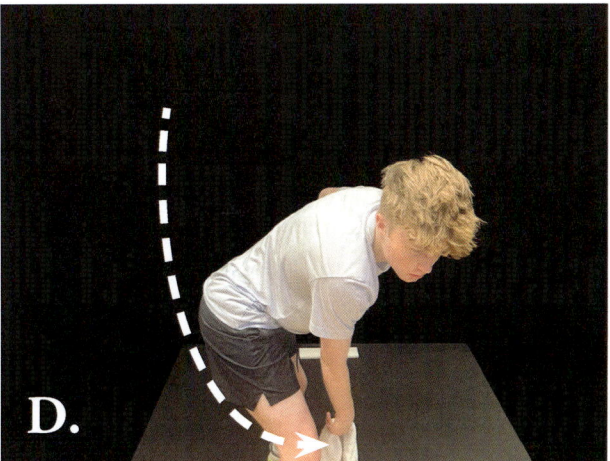

D.

29

DEVELOPING A PITCHER

TOWEL EXTENSION DRILL   ▪ 10 Reps

Why it's a good drill...

The Towel Extension Drill blends aspects of the Chest Over Knee Drill and the Glove-Side Tuck Drill into a single-fluid movement pattern. This drill helps pitchers avoid finishing across their body by promoting proper extension and encouraging full stride length.

Scan for Video Tutorial of Drill

> **EXPLAINED:** (A) Place an object (e.g., a chair, bucket, or bench) at a safe distance out in front of the pitching rubber. Holding the middle of a wrapped towel in the throwing hand, start by performing the 4-Step Windup. (B) At STEP #3 of the 4-Step Windup, think about the Separation Drill and begin to separate the hands into a "glove-side high" position at the same time the lifted leg drives to the ground. (C) As the body drives forward, pull the glove into the chest and down into the armpit. (D) Extend the throwing arm (and towel) as much as possible while trying to reach the object. Avoid positioning the object too close, or the throwing hand may hit it. Work hard to maximize reach by increasing the stride length over time.

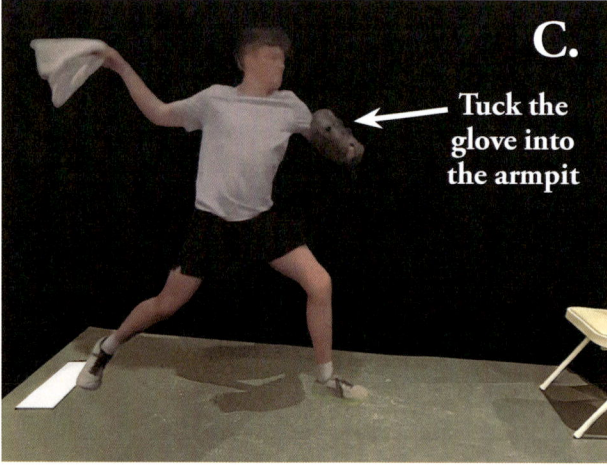

Helpful Tips & Caveats for Instructing the Drills

Good coaching involves being able to individualize training for a particular athlete at a given time. As an example, one athlete may require more repetitions to master a particular drill than another. If so, the instructor should adjust the recommended repetitions accordingly.

When working with players on the Separation Drill, we have found it helpful to place players in front of a mirror (or just a reflective window). The athletes can better see the "W" motion that their hands make, and the end result of finishing the drill with their "glove-side high."

Once an athlete has clearly mastered the first 4 drills, we've had success blending them together as a single drill. This enables more time to be devoted to the last 3 drills in a given training session. The **Blended Drill** results in the player starting with the 4-Step Windup, balancing at STEP #3, separating the hands in synchrony with the lifted leg moving downward, returning the hands back up in a "W" motion, and finishing with the front plant foot in-line with the back foot. Just note that a player cannot begin to blend these drills together until the player has first mastered each drill individually.

When incorporating the Blended Drill, we have players perform 20 repetitions of it first. Then, we have players complete each of the last 3 drills with additional repetitions (i.e., 15-20 each). When more repetitions are done with the Towel Extension Drill, we have players try and extend their stride length ever so slightly, while still appropriately tucking the glove (and not flying open) as they push off more with the back leg.

We add an additional **Arm Slot Drill** for players whose "natural" throwing motion looks out of sync. This usually occurs when a player is found, by slow motion video analysis, to have premature elbow extension (i.e., elbow angle greater than 90°) when the front plant foot *first touches* the ground. If this is present and the throwing elbow is <u>at or below</u> the throwing shoulder (Figure 4.1), we assign Arm Slot Drill Type 1. If this is present and the throwing elbow is <u>above</u> the throwing shoulder (Figure 4.2), we assign Arm Slot Drill Type 2. Please see the following two pages for more details about these drills.

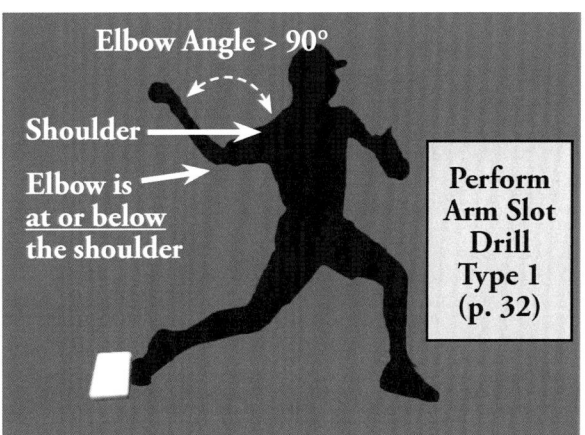

Figure 4.1

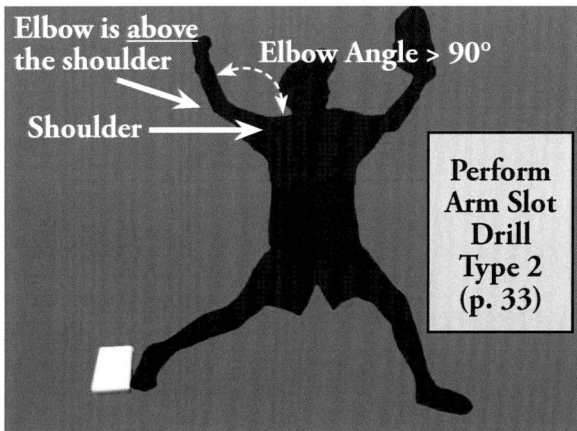

Figure 4.2

DEVELOPING A PITCHER

ARM SLOT DRILL TYPE 1

- 20 Reps w/ Club
- 20 Reps w/ Baseball
- 10 Reps Each (Throwing both w/ and w/o the Yellow Ball)

When to use it...

To improve throwing mechanics if a player has premature elbow extension (i.e., elbow flexion greater than 90°) at the time the front plant foot first touches the ground AND the throwing elbow is <u>at or below</u> the throwing shoulder (see image to the right).

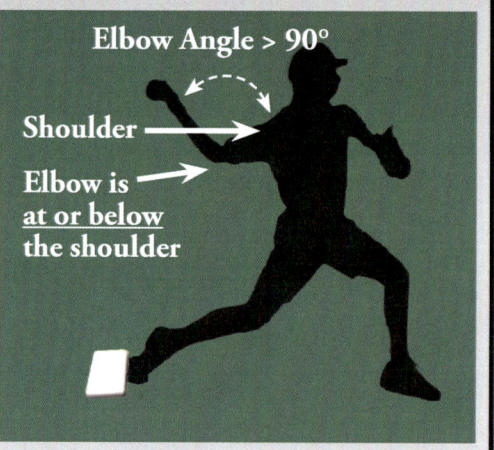

Scan for Video Tutorial of Drill

> **EXPLAINED:** (A) Hold the club in a "high-cocked" position with the yellow (TAP) ball positioned as shown. (B and C) Rotate the club over the head, keeping the TAP ball squeezed in place, close to the ear. Perform reps while: (1) holding the club, (2) holding the baseball, (3) holding and throwing the baseball into a net (TAP ball will dislodge from its position with each throw), and (4) throwing the baseball with <u>no</u> TAP ball present, but *imagining* it is there.

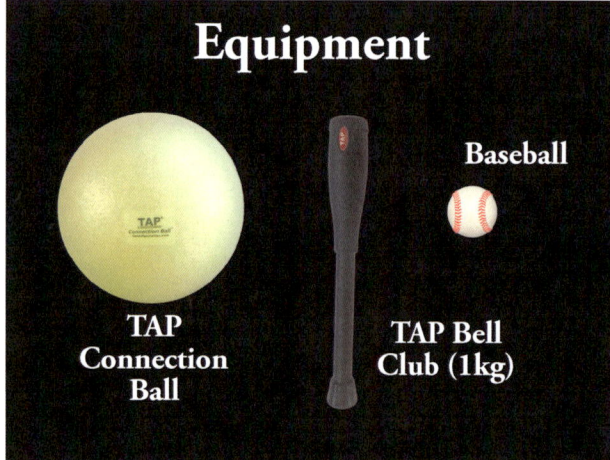

ARM SLOT DRILL TYPE 2

- 20 Reps w/ Club
- 20 Reps w/ Baseball
- 10 Reps Each (Throwing both w/ and w/o the Yellow Ball)

When to use it...

To improve throwing mechanics if a player has premature elbow extension (i.e., elbow flexion greater than 90°) at the time the front plant foot first touches the ground AND the throwing elbow is <u>above</u> the throwing shoulder (see image to the right).

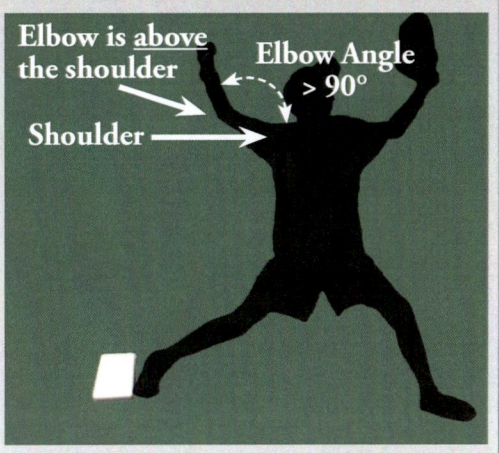

Scan for Video Tutorial of Drill

> **EXPLAINED:** (A) Hold the club in a "high-cocked" position with the yellow (TAP) ball positioned as shown. (B and C) Rotate the club over the head, keeping the TAP ball squeezed in place, under the armpit. Perform reps while: (1) holding the club, (2) holding the baseball, (3) holding & throwing the baseball into a net (TAP ball will dislodge from its position with each throw), and (4) throwing the baseball with <u>no</u> TAP ball present, but *imagining* it is there.

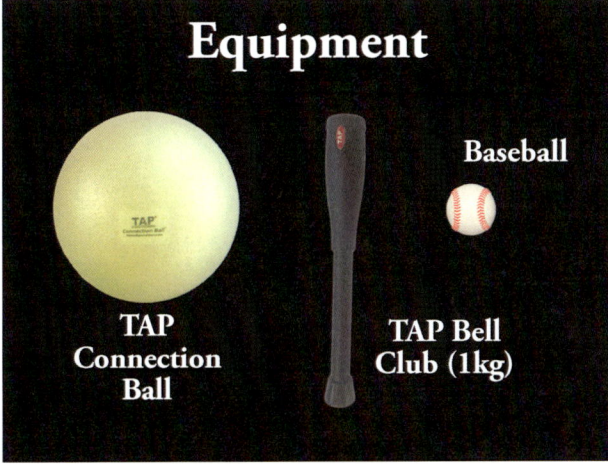

5
Equipment for Pitchers

> **Your equipment must be the best.
> That is how you will win victories.**
> —Gene Kranz
> *Chief Flight Director, NASA*

Once youth players have been consistent in performing the *Learning to Throw* routine and the *Learning to Pitch* drills over several seasons, they will have proven their interest in the sport, and they are now ready to enter the next phase in their development. This phase will require more investment in time and training resources, and in this chapter, we will focus our attention on the latter.

Baseball pitching training aids are now numerous with more and more devices coming to market every year. The industry is daunting to navigate for beginners and costly for players and their families. For this reason, some direction is needed, especially at the onset. At the time of this writing, we generate no

DEVELOPING A PITCHER

net income for ourselves from the sales of any training resources. We, like you, are predominantly consumers of these products, with years of experience integrating them into our methods.

We like to say that we have researched or used nearly everything on the market *once*, and we will continue to do so as long as we train our athletes. Our experience has taught us that novel products that truly lead to better and more efficient ways of training athletes come around far less frequently than the industry's marketing executives will lead you to believe. For this reason, we always approach new devices with a healthy degree of skepticism until they have shown to positively improve our client's experience or the performance measures that we monitor.

The equipment recommendations provided below have been *carefully* selected. By no means are they meant to be all-inclusive or represent the *only* things that might be helpful for developing a particular pitcher at a given time. These are just the items that we have found to generate the most success with our players. They collectively serve as the mainstay of our training approach.

We take pride in the conciseness of the list. Items that we have personally tested over the years and found to be "gimmicky" training aids have been weeded out. Items that have proven to be effective, durable, and add quality to player development, remain.

The equipment information is presented in color-coded fashion on the pages to follow. Equipment and devices that are labeled in GREEN represent the items that we feel should be prioritized as the basic necessities (and generally they will have lower cost). Equipment and devices labeled in SILVER have more specialized uses, and they can be prioritized secondarily. Equipment and devices labeled in GOLD are the most specialized tools and typically come with the highest costs. These items are primarily reserved for the most dedicated athletes.

understanding the labels...

GREEN
the basic necessities

Prioritize First

SILVER
more specialized items

Prioritize Secondarily

GOLD
most specialized tools

For the Most Dedicated

Equipment for Pitchers

Plyo Balls (Various Weights)

when we use them...
- For our *Arm Care & Velo Program* (Chapter 6).
- We get 3 of the 5 ounce (oz) "Purple" balls per player, because this is the weight of the standard baseball, and we throw them a lot!

where we get them...
Black (2000 g) ball is from DrivelineBaseball.com. All other balls are from OatesSpecialties.com.

1 - Black (4.4 lb or 2000 g)
1 - Green (32 oz)
1 - Blue (21 oz)
1 - Yellow (14 oz)
1 - Red (7 oz)
3 - Purple (5 oz)

Wrist Weights

10 lb

5 lb

when we use them...
- For the cooldown portion of our *Arm Care & Velo Program* (Chapter 6).
- You can start with the 5 lb wrist weights, and then as your strength and size increases, add the 10 lb wrist weights.

where we get them...
From DrivelineBaseball.com.

2 - 10 lb Wrist Weights
2 - 5 lb Wrist Weights

Arm Bands

when we use them...
- For our *Arm Care & Velo Program* (Chapter 6).
- Get an age-appropriate band size. If from Oates Specialties: Blue (middle school), Black (high school), or Silver (well-developed high school).

where we get them...
From OatesSpecialties.com.

DEVELOPING A PITCHER

Foam Roller

when we use it...

- For the warm-up routine prior to any throwing and strength training days.
- We like the high-density (i.e., "harder") foam roller of 36" in length.

where we get it...

Amazon Basics High-Density Foam Roller from Amazon.com.

Wrapped Towel

when we use it...

- For our *Learning to Pitch* drills (Chapter 4).
- Any thin or small towel about 2 ft in length will do. Place athletic tape around the middle to serve as the location for your grip.

where we get it...

Just use an old towel from around the house.

"Blue" Exercise Balance Pad

when we use it...

- To support the knee when throwing plyo balls from the ground.
- We like the 15.5" length x 12.75" width x 2.25" thick pad.

where we get it...

ProsourceFit Exercise Balance Pad from Amazon.com.

38

EQUIPMENT FOR PITCHERS | 5

Plyo Wall

when we use it...
- For the plyo ball portions of our *Arm Care & Velo Program* (Chapter 6).
- The plyo wall is used with the plyo balls, while the sock net below is used with real baseballs.
- We place a handle on the side to attach bands.

where we get it...
We build it with wood, horse trailer mats, & caster wheels; Internet search "DIY plyo wall" for ideas.

Sock Net

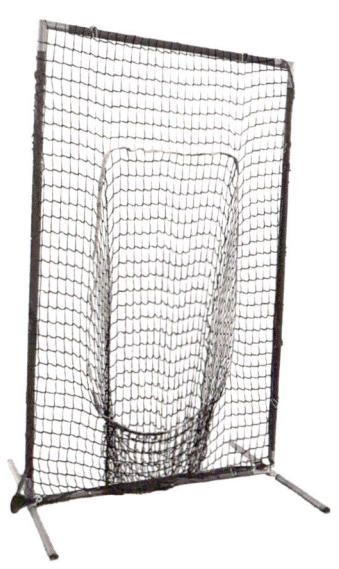

when we use it...
- For our *Arm Care & Velo Program* (Chapter 6).
- The sock net is used when we throw real baseballs, while the plyo wall above is used when we throw plyo balls.

where we get it...
Many brands have budget friendly options; we get ours with wheels from MuhlTech.com and it lasts.

Plyo Wall & Sock Net Alternatives

You will find it very difficult to become a successful high school pitcher without access to a plyo wall and sock net (or equivalent). Pitchers must consistently throw as a part of their arm care and will not always have someone available to catch for them, making these items critical for self-motivated progress.

You can get creative to make things work at minimal cost, if necessary. Many Little League complexes and parks provide public access to batting cages and/or nets, and there are portable plyo mats available (see image to the right) that can easily be hung on a chain link fence. That said, if there is ever anything to invest in to become a pitcher, it is the basic pitching necessities that we have outlined here.

TAP Portable Plyo Mat
From OatesSpecialties.com

DEVELOPING A PITCHER

TAP Training Sock

when we use it...

- For performing throwing drills indoors, on the go (traveling), or even at team practices.
- The device also develops posterior shoulder strength, through weighted deceleration of the arm, following the ball's release inside the sock.

where we get it...

From OatesSpecialties.com.

Core Velocity Belt

when we use it...

- For our *Arm Care & Velo Program* (Chapter 6).
- The device attaches to the thighs and waist, and connects to a bungee cord, which helps to naturally "pull" the hips through on delivery.

where we get it...

From CoreVelocityBelt.com.

Portolite Pitching Mound

when we use it...

- For our *Arm Care & Velo Program* and *Bullpen Pitching* (Chapters 6 and 7).
- This is the biggest investment in this category, but Portolite makes durable products that will survive the outdoor elements for years!

where we get it...

From Portolite.com (1-piece and 2-piece practice mounds are available).

TAP Connection Ball

when we use it...

- For our *Learning to Pitch* drills (Chapter 4).
- This item has specialized use only, but if throwing mechanics need to be modified, it is an invaluable tool for the arm slot drills.

where we get it...

From OatesSpecialties.com.

TAP Bell Club

when we use it...

- For our *Learning to Pitch* drills (Chapter 4).
- This item has specialized use only, but if throwing mechanics need to be modified, it is an invaluable tool for the arm slot drills.

where we get it...

From OatesSpecialties.com.

1 kg
(2.2 lb)

Pitcher's Pocket Pro 9 Hole Net

when we use it...

- For *Bullpen Pitching* (Chapter 7).
- The older you get, the more days you will have when a catcher is unavailable to help you get better. Don't let that be an excuse!

where we get it...

From BetterBaseball.com.

DEVELOPING A PITCHER

Marc Pro

when we use it...

- For recovery (instead of icing the arm) after high-intensity throwing days and game performances.
- Many of our pitchers have solved their arm and muscle soreness issues with it.

where we get it...

From MarcPro.com.

Radar with Display

when we use it...

- For our *Arm Care & Velo Program* (Chapter 6).
- If you want to run faster, you need to invest in a timer; if you want to throw harder, you will ultimately benefit from a radar.

where we get it...

Radar Cube from JugsSports.com, or Smart Coach Bundle with Display from PocketRadar.com.

Handheld Percussive Device

when we use it...

- For warm-up and recovery (before and after training).
- Specifically following the foam roller to warm up large muscle groups prior to strength training, and post workout for any knots.

where we get it...

Many brands are available, but we get ours from Therabody.com.

EQUIPMENT FOR PITCHERS | 5

Home Gym Equipment

when we use it...
- For our *Strength Program* (Chapter 8).
- This is the largest investment in this category, but if used consistently, the upside is huge. It improves the likelihood that strength training can be done at the busiest times of the year.

where we get it...
From RogueFitness.com and AncoreTraining.com.

Recommended Items Pictured Above...

- **Rack with pair of J-Cups and Safety Straps** *From RogueFitness.com*
- **Flat Utility Bench** *From RogueFitness.com*
- **45 lb Bar (or 22 lb Bar for younger ages)** *From RogueFitness.com*
- **Vertical Weight Tree** *From RogueFitness.com*
- **Bumper Plates (weights)** *From RogueFitness.com*
- **Ancore Pro (portable cable machine)** *From AncoreTraining.com*

Rapsodo with Insight Camera

when we use it...
- Rapsodo: For pitch velocity and spin rate.
- Insight Camera: For self-awareness of finger positioning at ball release on each pitch-type.
- For player portfolio data collection for our high school pitchers that are college/pro prospects.

where we get it...
From Rapsodo.com.

6
Arm Care & Velo Program

> "
> Discipline gets you beat more than
> great helps you win.
> —Kelvin Sampson

The main purpose of a throwing program is to build velocity and reduce the likelihood of injury. This is done by conditioning the arm to better withstand the forces that will be placed upon it. The benefits achieved from a throwing program will mostly come from being able to perform the program *consistently*, which means it must be well-designed for sustainability throughout the adolescent and high school years.

We have generally found that the greatest gains in velocity (and strength) throughout the year occur during the off-season. Players can more consistently complete daily workout routines when their schedules are not impacted by the need to be ready for unpredictable pitching appearances in games and tournament play.

DEVELOPING A PITCHER

For this reason, our *Arm Care & Velo Program* is specifically designed with the off-season in mind. This is where it provides the ideal structure to build arm strength, improve mechanics, and increase throwing velocity. What sets it apart, however, is its versatility—it can be seamlessly adapted for in-season or year-round use with only minor adjustments, allowing pitchers to maintain gains and stay healthy no matter where they are in their training cycle.

You might find it surprising that our program does not include a formal "long toss" routine. While there is some debate[1] on both the safety and effectiveness of long toss (which generates different shoulder rotation angles and release points relative to throwing off the mound), we do not want to imply that it has no role. In fact, the majority of our in-season team practice plans incorporate a long toss regimen, and on some days in the off-season, our pitchers will perform long toss in lieu of *Bullpen* (or *Flat-Ground*) *Pitching* (to be discussed in Chapter 7).

....

[1] Boddy, K. "The Facts Behind Long Toss Training in Baseball." Driveline Baseball, https://www.drivelinebaseball.com/2013/01/the-facts-behind-long-toss. Accessed 4/1/2025.

We mainly want to emphasize that a defining characteristic of our *Arm Care & Velo Program* is that it can be done in smaller spaces. True long toss routines require large fields (or at least very tall nets) and added time for players to travel to and from complexes. We have found that the closer you can bring your training environment to your home, the more likely it is to get done.

Program Components

Our *Arm Care & Velo Program* is comprised of 3 primary components: the warm-up, the throwing phase, and the cooldown (Figure 6.1). In this chapter, we will first explain the activities in the order in which they are performed by our pitchers. The number of repetitions or time recommended for each activity is only meant to serve as a guide and may vary for individual athletes based upon physicality and specific training goals. Since *simplicity* matters for *sustainability*, you will find that our program is generally the same for the off-season and the pre-season. Later in the chapter, we will explain how it is modified slightly for bullpen pitching days (at any time of the year), and once in-season team practice and throwing activities begin.

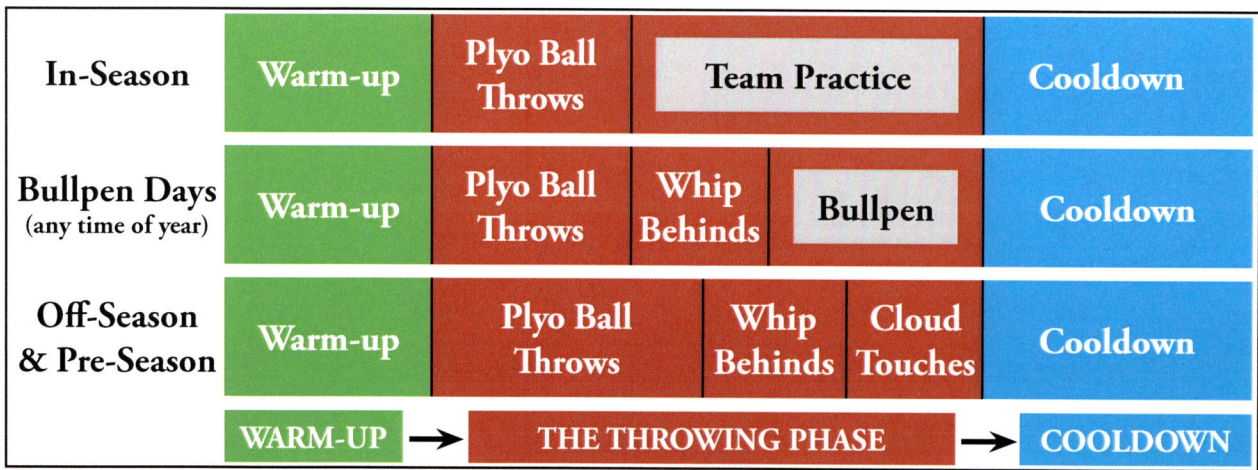

Figure 6.1 - Arm Care & Velo Program Overview

MYOFASCIAL RELEASE (ROLL OUT)

WARM-UP

What you will do...

- Back (60 seconds)
- Glutes, Hamstrings, and Calves (60 seconds)
- Quadriceps and Groin/Adductors (90 seconds)
- Latissimus Dorsi, Deltoids, and Lateral Chest (90 seconds)

Scan for Visual of Roll Out

> (A) Begin with the foam roller by rolling out the lower, middle, and upper back. (B) Proceed to the glutes, hamstrings, and calves. (C) Turn over and face the chest to the ground. Roll out the quadriceps. (D) Bend one leg at the knee and roll out the groin/adductors. (E) Roll out the latissimus dorsi and deltoids. (F) Finish by rolling out the lateral chest.

A.

B.

C.

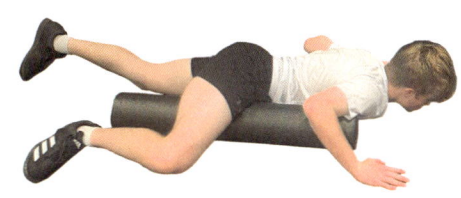

D. *Perform on both legs.

E. *Perform on both sides.

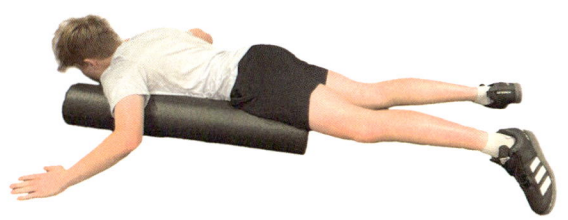

F. *Perform on both sides.

DEVELOPING A PITCHER

ARM BANDS

What you will do...

10 REPETITIONS OF EACH OF THE FOLLOWING:
- Elevated Internal Rotation (Forward Goal Posts)
- Elevated External Rotation (Reverse Goal Posts)
- Forward Flies (Forward "T")

Scan for Visual of Arm Bands

Elevated Internal Rotation [Forward Goal Posts] (10 Reps)

With the bands attached from behind and the elbows bent at 90°, raise the elbows to the level of the shoulder ("goal posts"). Rotate the hands forward to internally rotate the shoulder. Return to the starting position.

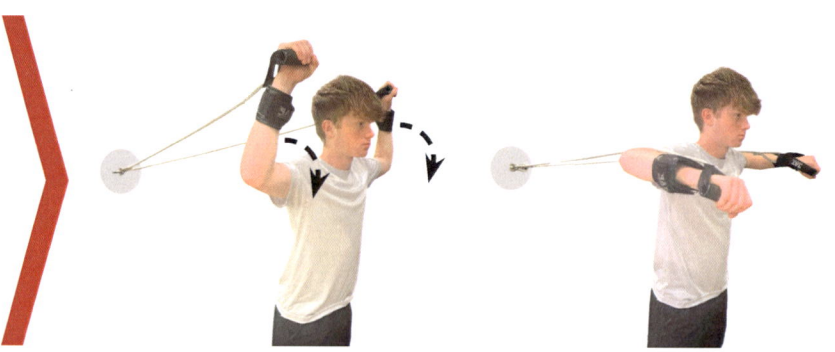

Elevated External Rotation [Reverse Goal Posts] (10 Reps)

With the bands attached out in front and the elbows bent at 90°, raise the elbows to shoulder level. Rotate the hands backward to externally rotate the shoulder (into "goal posts"). Return to the starting position.

Forward Flies [Forward "T"] (10 Reps)

With the bands attached from behind and the arms straight out to the side ("T" position), bring both hands together directly in front. Return to the starting position.

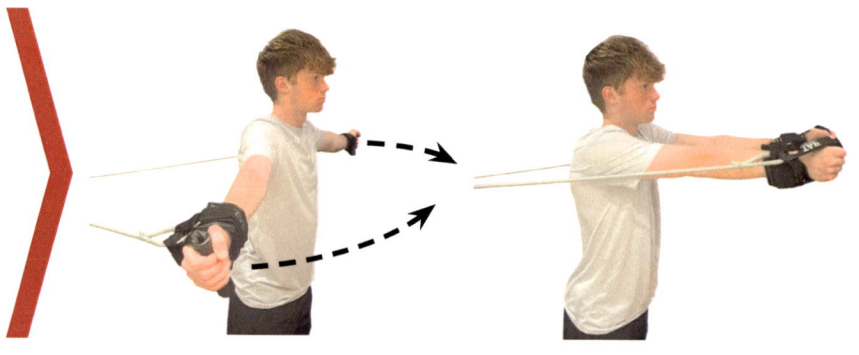

WARM-UP

What you will do...

10 REPETITIONS OF EACH OF THE FOLLOWING:

- Reverse Flies (Reverse "T")
- Internal Rotation at Hip (Both Arms Individually)
- External Rotation at Hip (Both Arms Individually)

Reverse Flies [Reverse "T"] (10 Reps)

With the bands attached out in front and the arms extended straight with both hands together, pull the arms straight to the side ("T" position) and as far back as possible. Return to the starting position.

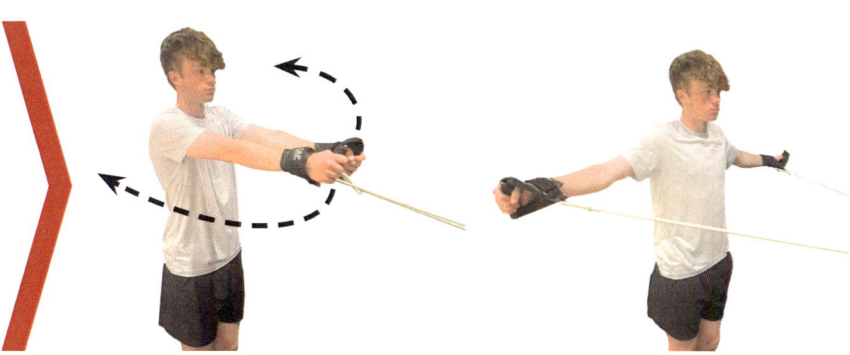

Internal Rotation at Hip [Both Arms] (10 Reps)

With the bands attached on the same side as the arm being worked, lock the elbow at 90° just above the hip. Move the hand toward the abdomen to internally rotate the shoulder. Return to the starting position.

External Rotation at Hip [Both Arms] (10 Reps)

With the bands attached on the opposite side of the arm being worked, lock the elbow at 90° just above the hip. Move the hand away from the abdomen to externally rotate the shoulder. Return to the starting position.

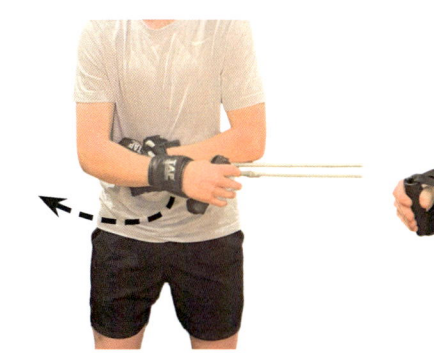

DEVELOPING A PITCHER

ARM BANDS (CONT.)   WARM-UP

What you will do...

10 REPETITIONS OF EACH OF THE FOLLOWING:
- Standing "Y"
- Back Rows
- Statue of Liberty (30 second stretch, single repetition)

Standing "Y" (10 Reps)

With the bands attached out in front and the arms extended straight with both hands together, pull the arms up and back, without bending the elbows, into a "Y" formation. Return to the starting position.

Back Rows (10 Reps)

With the bands attached out in front and the arms extended straight with both hands together, pull the elbows back as far as possible. Return to the starting position.

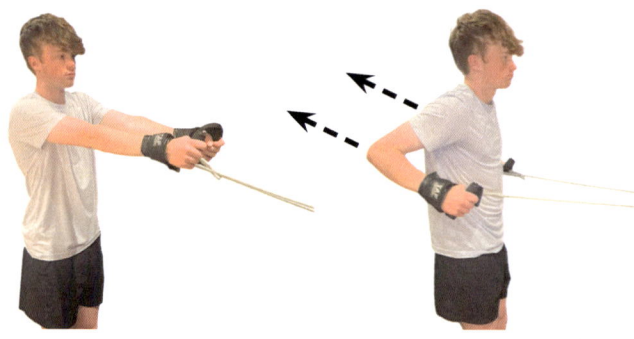

Statue of Liberty (30 Seconds)

With a single band attached from behind, raise the throwing arm to the release point and then slowly allow the shoulder to externally rotate back, bringing the arm behind the head to stretch the arm.

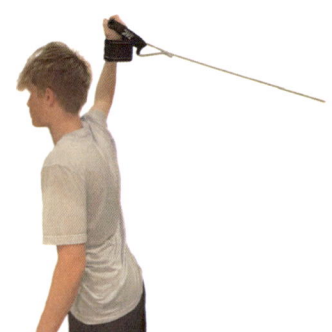

DYNAMIC WARM-UP ROUTINE (ABBREVIATED)

WARM-UP

What you will do...

- High Knees (30 ft x 2)
- Bottom Kickers (30 ft x 2)
- Knee Huggers (30 ft x 2)
- Cradle Walks (30 ft x 2)
- Lunges with Twist (30 ft x 2)
- Side Lunges (30 seconds)
- Groin Stretches (20 seconds x 2)

Scan for Visual

(Note: All of the activities below are outlined with images in Chapter 2.)

HIGH KNEES > Perform at a moderate pace. Jog linearly in the forward direction while bringing each knee above the waist and towards the chest. Pump the arms accordingly.
DISTANCE: 30 ft in one direction, rest briefly, then 30 ft back.

BOTTOM KICKERS > Perform at a moderate pace. Jog linearly in the forward direction, bending each knee backward so the heel can touch the bottom. The thigh should remain in a vertical position and not lift up toward the chest. Pump the arms accordingly.
DISTANCE: 30 ft in one direction, rest briefly, then 30 ft back.

KNEE HUGGERS > Perform at a very slow pace. Step with one leg, and then grab the knee of the opposite leg, bringing ("hugging") it up to the chest. Return the leg to the ground. Alternate legs while walking the distance.
DISTANCE: 30 ft in one direction, rest briefly, then 30 ft back.

CRADLE WALKS > Perform at a very slow pace. Step with one leg, and then grab the side of the opposite leg's foot, pulling ("cradling") it up to the waist. Return the leg to the ground. Alternate legs, back and forth, while walking the distance.
DISTANCE: 30 ft in one direction, rest briefly, then 30 ft back.

LUNGES W/ TWIST > Perform at a very slow pace. Step with one leg and bend the front knee, allowing the back knee to almost touch the ground. Hold that position and twist the upper torso from side to side. Alternate legs while walking the distance.
DISTANCE: 30 ft in one direction, rest briefly, then 30 ft back.

SIDE LUNGES > Perform slowly. Start with both legs straight and spread apart wide. Shift the body to one side, bending the knee while keeping the opposite leg straight. Shift the body to the other side. Repeat back and forth.
DURATION: 30 seconds.

GROIN STRETCHES > Squat down and place the elbows on the inside of the knees, and press outward with the legs providing resistance. Then, place the arms on the outside of the legs, and pull inward with the legs providing resistance.
DURATION: 20 seconds each for the elbows inside and outside the knees.

DEVELOPING A PITCHER

PLYO BALL THROWS - REVERSE THROWS

THROWING

What you will do...

10 REVERSE THROWS WITH EACH OF THE FOLLOWING:
- **32 ounce** Plyo Ball (Oates Specialties "Green" Ball)
- **21 ounce** Plyo Ball (Oates Specialties "Blue" Ball)

Scan for Visual of the Drill

> **EXPLAINED:** (A) Position the back to the plyo wall. (B1) Place the throwing side knee (i.e., the right knee for right-handed throwers) on the Blue Exercise Balance Pad. (B2) Throw the plyo ball in a "reverse" motion. The arm should pass through the same release point of a normal throw, and (B3) the chest should twist about 90° from the starting position as the throw is completed.

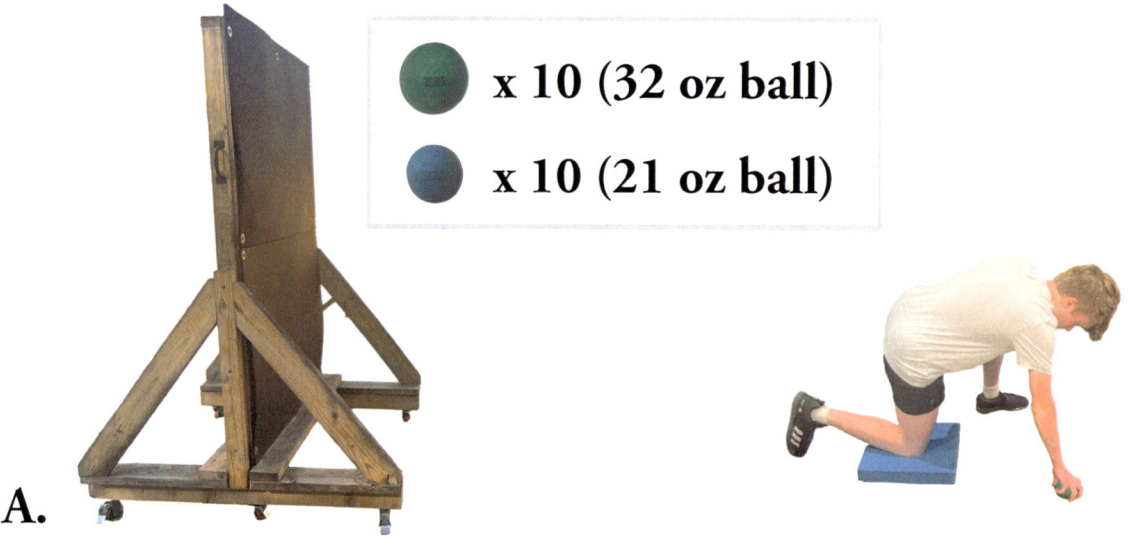

● x 10 (32 oz ball)
● x 10 (21 oz ball)

A.

B.

ARM CARE & VELO PROGRAM | 6

PLYO BALL THROWS - TWIST AND THROWS

THROWING

What you will do...

10 TWIST AND THROWS WITH EACH OF THE FOLLOWING:
- **21 ounce** Plyo Ball (Oates Specialties "Blue" Ball)
- **14 ounce** Plyo Ball (Oates Specialties "Yellow" Ball)

Scan for Visual of the Drill

> **EXPLAINED:** (A) Stand with the side of the throwing shoulder pointed toward the plyo wall. (B1) While keeping the feet anchored in the ground, (B2) twist the torso ≥ 90° so first the chest, and then the glove-side shoulder, faces the plyo wall. (B3 and B4) Throw the ball.

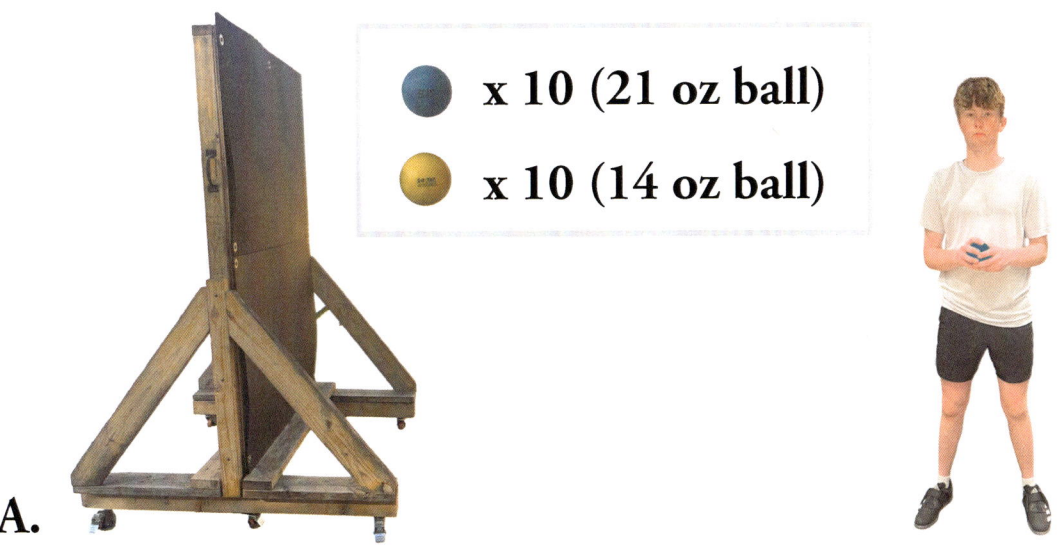

A.

B.

DEVELOPING A PITCHER

PLYO BALL THROWS - HIP FINISHERS

What you will do...

15 HIP FINISHERS (3 SETS OF 5) WITH THE FOLLOWING:

- **7 ounce** Plyo Ball (Oates Specialties "Red" Ball)*

*Note the Alternative Method (on the opposite page) to be used when a pitching mound and Core Velocity Belt are available.

Scan for Visual of the Drill

> **EXPLAINED:** (A and B1) Stand with the back foot and chest pointing toward the plyo wall. (B2) Rock back on the heel. (B3) Push off with the back toe. (B4) Internally rotate the back hip as it drives forward. (C) Think about rolling the back foot on top of the toes to better "feel" the internal rotation of the hip that's necessary for a more powerful delivery.

A.

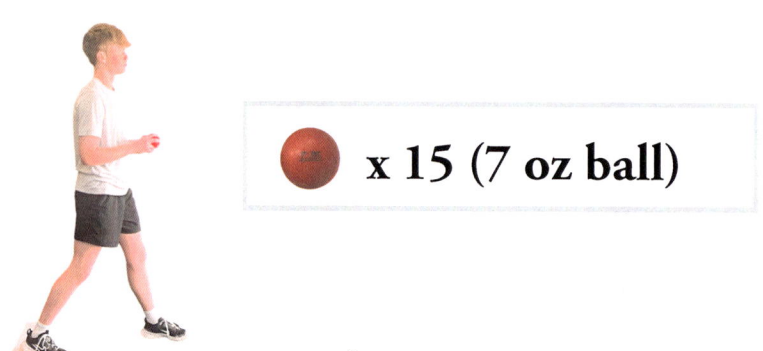

x 15 (7 oz ball)

B.

① ② ③ ④

C.

PUSH OFF — ROLL ON TOP OF TOES — INTERNALLY ROTATE BACK HIP FORWARD

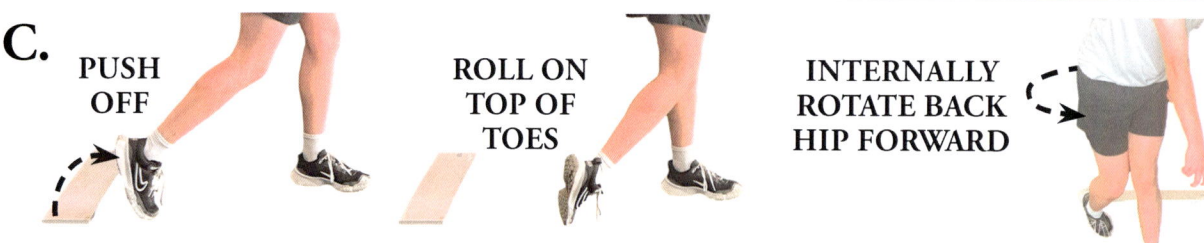

THROWING

ALTERNATIVE METHOD (HIP FINISHERS)

15 HIP FINISHERS (3 SETS OF 5) with the **7 ounce** Plyo Ball (Oates Specialties "Red" Ball):

- <u>1st Set of 5</u>
  Perform wearing the Core Velocity Belt with the "Black" (standard tension) band attached.
- <u>2nd Set of 5</u>
  Perform wearing the Core Velocity Belt with the "Blue" (heavier tension) band attached.
- <u>3rd Set of 5</u>
  Perform with <u>no tension band</u> attached (but keep the Core Velocity Belt on for the next drill).

By providing a subtle degree of tension on the hips/pelvis, the Core Velocity Belt helps pitchers "feel" more efficient movements of their lower half. The belt can be worn during most pitching drills, but we especially like to incorporate its use into our HIP FINISHERS and WEIGH MORES routines. We adjust tension bands between sets to provide alternating degrees of "feel," and then we remove the bands entirely on subsequent sets so the body can try to replicate the same movements without an external aid. More details regarding the use and application of the Core Velocity Belt can be found at CoreVelocityBelt.com.

> **EXPLAINED:** Wearing the Core Velocity Belt, place the back foot on the pitching mound rubber and perform the activity outlined on the opposite page (p. 54). Tension bands (when attached) for this drill will be hooked to the hip ring on the side of the throwing arm. "Feel" the hip move forward and internally rotate with each push-off of the back foot during the throw.

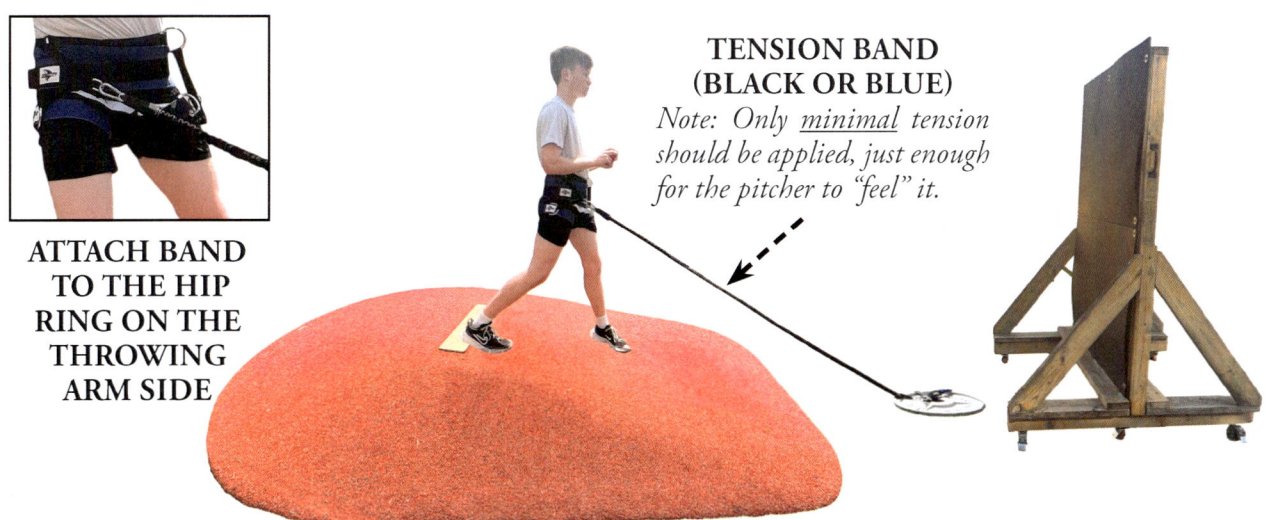

ATTACH BAND TO THE HIP RING ON THE THROWING ARM SIDE

TENSION BAND (BLACK OR BLUE)
Note: Only <u>minimal</u> tension should be applied, just enough for the pitcher to "feel" it.

DEVELOPING A PITCHER

PLYO BALL THROWS - WEIGH MORES

What you will do...

15 WEIGH MORES (3 SETS OF 5) WITH THE FOLLOWING:

- **5 ounce** Plyo Ball (Oates Specialties "Purple" Ball)*

*Note the Alternative Method (on the opposite page) to be used when a pitching mound and Core Velocity Belt are available.

Scan for Visual of the Drill

> **EXPLAINED:** (A and B1) Start from the pitcher's stretch position with the front shoulder pointing toward the plyo wall. (B2) Perform a standard leg lift. (B3) At the height of the leg lift, bend the back knee slightly and "sink," thinking about pushing as hard as possible into the ground with the back foot in order to "weigh more," and then make an explosive throw.

A.

 x 15 (5 oz ball)

B.

①

②

THINK ABOUT PUSHING INTO THE GROUND WITH THE BACK FOOT TO "WEIGH MORE"

③

ALTERNATIVE METHOD (WEIGH MORES)

15 WEIGH MORES (3 SETS OF 5) with the **5 ounce** Plyo Ball (Oates Specialties "Purple" Ball):

- <u>1st Set of 5</u>
  Perform wearing the Core Velocity Belt with the "Black" (standard tension) band attached.
- <u>2nd Set of 5</u>
  Perform wearing the Core Velocity Belt with the "Blue" (heavier tension) band attached.
- <u>3rd Set of 5</u>
  Perform with <u>no tension band</u> attached (the Core Velocity Belt can now be entirely removed).

By providing a subtle degree of tension on the hips/pelvis, the Core Velocity Belt helps pitchers "feel" more efficient movements of their lower half. The belt can be worn during most pitching drills, but we especially like to incorporate its use into our HIP FINISHERS and WEIGH MORES routines. We adjust tension bands between sets to provide alternating degrees of "feel," and then we remove the bands entirely on subsequent sets so the body can try to replicate the same movements without an external aid. More details regarding the use and application of the Core Velocity Belt can be found at CoreVelocityBelt.com.

> **EXPLAINED:** Wearing the Core Velocity Belt, place the back foot on the pitching mound rubber and perform the activity outlined on the opposite page (p. 56). Tension bands (when attached) for this drill will be passed through the front hip loop and attached to the back hip ring. "Feel" the hip pull forward and rotate internally with each throw.

BAND PASSES THROUGH THE FRONT HIP LOOP AND ATTACHES TO THE BACK HIP RING

TENSION BAND (BLACK OR BLUE)
Note: Only <u>minimal</u> tension should be applied, just enough for the pitcher to "feel" it.

DEVELOPING A PITCHER

WHIP BEHINDS

THROWING

What you will do...

10 WHIP BEHINDS WITH THE FOLLOWING:

- Standard Baseball (**5 ounce**)*

*If available, place the Radar Cube (or equivalent) 15 ft behind the net to provide velocity feedback with each throw.

Scan for Visual of the Drill

> **EXPLAINED:** (A and B1) As explained in Chapter 3, stand with the feet spread apart wide. (B2) Whip the back leg behind the front leg and spring the body forward in a linear direction. (B3) Throw the ball. The distance from the back foot's starting point to the *spring-forward point* (A) should be approximately twice the width of the player's initial stance.

A.

x 10 (standard 5 oz baseball)

⇢ SPRING-FORWARD POINT

B.

① ② ③

IN AN EXPLOSIVE MANNER, WHIP THE BACK FOOT BEHIND THE FRONT LEG AND THROW

CLOUD TOUCHES

THROWING

What you will do...

10 CLOUD TOUCHES WITH THE FOLLOWING:

- Standard Baseball (**5 ounce**)*

*If available, place the Radar Cube (or equivalent) 15 ft behind the net to provide velocity feedback with each throw.

Scan for Visual of the Drill

> **EXPLAINED:** (A and B1) As explained in Chapter 3, start from a standing position and get a 5-10 ft running start. (B) Use either a "crow hop" or a leg "whip behind" prior to releasing the ball. (B3) As the hands separate to initiate the throw, focus on getting the glove (or glove-side shoulder) pointed upward to the sky ("cloud touches"). (B4) Throw the ball.

A.

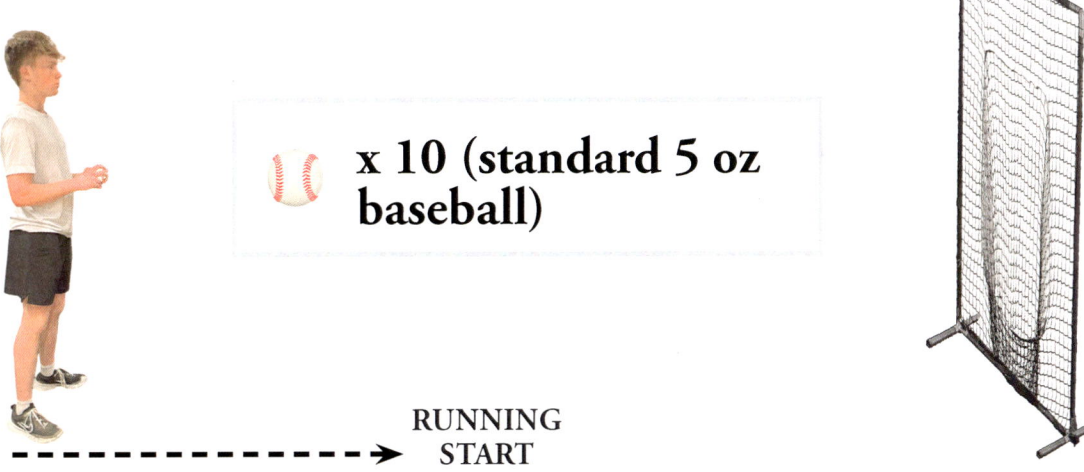

x 10 (standard 5 oz baseball)

RUNNING START

B.

GET FRONT SHOULDER HIGH TO THE SKY ("CLOUD TOUCHES")

① ② ③ ④

DEVELOPING A PITCHER

WRIST WEIGHTS & HEAVY PLYO BALL

What you will do...

ONE SET OF EACH OF THE FOLLOWING:
- Presses (60 seconds) with **5 lb** Wrist Weights
- Bent-Over Rows (50 reps) with **5 lb** Wrist Weights
- Rotational Presses (25 reps) with **5 lb** Wrist Weights

Scan for Visual of Cooldown

Presses (60 Seconds)

With 5 lb wrist weights on each wrist and elbows bent at 90° at the level of the shoulder ("goal posts"), press both hands upward. Return to the starting position and repeat.

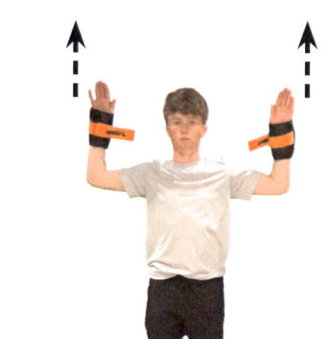

Bent-Over Rows (50 Reps)

With 5 lb wrist weights on each wrist and knees bent, chest leaning forward, and arms straight, pull both elbows back as far as possible. Return to the starting position and repeat.

Rotational Presses (25 Reps)

With 5 lb wrist weights on each wrist, elbows bent at 90°, and internally rotated shoulders, move into the "goal posts" position and then press upward. Return back down in sequence and repeat.

COOLDOWN

What you will do...

ONE SET OF EACH OF THE FOLLOWING:
- Elevated Arm Hold (60 seconds) with **10 lb** Wrist Weight
- Horizontal Ball Hold (60 seconds) with **4.4 lb (2000 g)** Plyo Ball (Driveline "Black" Ball)
- Kneeling Ball Hold (60 seconds) with **4.4 lb (2000 g)** Plyo Ball (Driveline "Black" Ball)

Elevated Arm Hold (60 Seconds)

With a 10 lb wrist weight on the throwing arm wrist, raise the hand upward to a high release point position (with the elbow slightly bent), and hold it in place for the duration.

Horizontal Ball Hold (60 seconds)

Grip a 4.4 lb (2000 g) plyo ball with the throwing hand on top of the ball. Straighten the elbow, and place the outstretched arm in a horizontal position (as shown). Hold it in place for the duration.

Kneeling Ball Hold (60 seconds)

With a 4.4 lb (2000 g) plyo ball in the throwing hand, kneel on the throwing side knee, and raise the hand upward to a high release point position (with the elbow slightly bent). Hold it in place for the duration.

DEVELOPING A PITCHER

Off-Season & Pre-Season

The program explained on the preceding pages is summarized in Table 6.1 (see right). Once pitchers are familiar with its movements and sequencing, it can be completed in under 40 minutes. We recommend performing this program 3 times per week in the **off-season** and maintaining the same weekly frequency throughout the **pre-season** (which we define as the 4 weeks leading up to the start of a new season).

When it's performed during the off-season and the pre-season, the *Arm Care & Velo Program* is structured to have only **one variation**, and this occurs when minor adjustments are made on *Bullpen Pitching* days. To account for the increased throwing volume, Weigh Mores and Cloud Touches are eliminated from the program on bullpen days to avoid overloading. Table 6.2 (see opposite page) summarizes this one variation.

Bullpen Pitching (or its occasional substitute, *Flat-Ground Pitching*) and strength training are to be discussed in upcoming chapters, so their programming details are not included here—aside from noting that their recommended weekly frequency changes throughout the year, as shown in the following table:

Program Days Per Week (By Season)			
	Arm Care & Velo	Bullpen (or FGP*)	Strength Training
Off-Season	3	1	3
Pre-Season	3	2	3
*FGP = Flat-Ground Pitching			

Arm Care & Velo
Non-Bullpen Pitching Day

WARM-UP
Myofascial Release (Roll Out)
Arm Bands
Dynamic Warm-up / Stretch

THROWING
Plyo Ball - Reverse Throws
    32 oz ball x 10 reps
    21 oz ball x 10 reps
Plyo Ball - Twist & Throws
    21 oz ball x 10 reps
    14 oz ball x 10 reps
Plyo Ball - Hip Finishers
    7 oz ball, 3 sets x 5 reps
Plyo Ball - Weigh Mores
    5 oz ball, 3 sets x 5 reps
Whip Behinds
    Baseball (5 oz) x 10 reps
Cloud Touches
    Baseball (5 oz) x 10 reps

COOLDOWN
5 lb Wrist Weights
    Presses x 60 secs
    Bent-Over Rows x 50 reps
    Rotational Presses x 25 reps
10 lb Wrist Weights
    Elevated Arm Hold x 60 secs
4.4 lb (2000 g) Plyo Ball
    Horizontal Ball Hold x 60 secs
    Kneeling Ball Hold x 60 secs

Table 6.1

Since *Bullpen Pitching* always occurs on a scheduled *Arm Care & Velo Program* day, a sample **off-season** routine, with 1 weekly bullpen and 3 strength training days, would look something like the following:

WEEKLY OFF-SEASON ROUTINE

In the example above, Table 6.1 outlines the *Arm Care & Velo Program* for Mondays and Wednesdays (non-bullpen days), while Table 6.2 outlines the program for Fridays (bullpen days).

Likewise, a sample **pre-season** routine, with 2 weekly bullpens and 3 strength training days, would look something like the following:

WEEKLY PRE-SEASON ROUTINE

Arm Care & Velo
Bullpen Pitching Day

WARM-UP

Myofascial Release (Roll Out)

Arm Bands

Dynamic Warm-up / Stretch

THROWING

Plyo Ball - Reverse Throws

32 oz ball x 10 reps

21 oz ball x 10 reps

Plyo Ball - Twist & Throws

21 oz ball x 10 reps

14 oz ball x 10 reps

Plyo Ball - Hip Finishers

7 oz ball, 3 sets x 5 reps

Whip Behinds

Baseball (5 oz) x 10 reps

BULLPEN PITCHING ROUTINE
(See Chapter 7)

COOLDOWN

5 lb Wrist Weights

Presses x 60 secs

Bent-Over Rows x 50 reps

Rotational Presses x 25 reps

10 lb Wrist Weights

Elevated Arm Hold x 60 secs

4.4 lb (2000 g) Plyo Ball

Horizontal Ball Hold x 60 secs

Kneeling Ball Hold x 60 secs

Table 6.2

DEVELOPING A PITCHER

In-Season

The second and **final variation** of the *Arm Care & Velo Program* occurs **in-season**. In our experience, this is the most difficult time of the year for pitchers to maintain consistency. Team practices and games present an environment that often is unpredictable for a pitcher. Moreover, while every team practice plan *should* incorporate all basic components of arm care (warm-up, throwing, and cooldown), this is not always a guarantee, or something an individual player can necessarily control.

Adding to the complexity is that pitchers will not always know the games in which they will be asked to pitch. They will frequently have to be "ready" to throw on some days when they will never end up pitching. This uncertainty creates obvious challenges. Pitchers who have not previously developed a self-disciplined approach to their arm care and other programs will be most susceptible to failure.

Table 6.3 (see opposite page) summarizes the modified *Arm Care & Velo Program* for the **in-season**. This program should be performed on all team activity days (e.g., practices and games), as depicted in the following table, which outlines the recommended number of days per week of all **in-season** routines:

Program Days Per Week (By Season)			
	Arm Care & Velo†	Bullpen (or FGP*)	Strength Training
In-Season	5	2	2

†Only involves warm-up and cooldown (Table 6.3) on all team activity days
*FGP = Flat-Ground Pitching

The variation made **in-season** to the *Arm Care & Velo Program* is that it's reduced to a routine of **warm-up** and **cooldown** activities only. These components of arm care are usually the most lacking in team practice plans. Some degree of high-intensity throwing will usually be taking place during team activities, but pitchers will frequently need to take self-ownership of their own warm-up and cooldown exercises.

This means if the warm-up at a team practice is underemphasized, pitchers should have their own set of arm bands in their baseball equipment

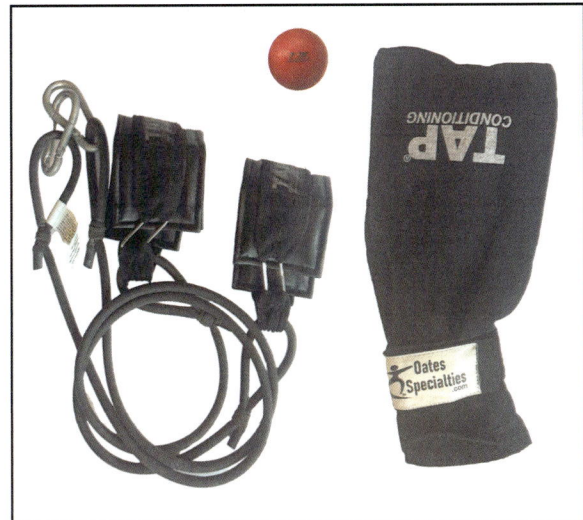

Figure 6.2 - Baseball Bag Equipment

bag, along with the TAP Baseball Training Sock, and a 7 oz plyo ball (Figure 6.2). When practical, pitchers should arrive early to practice and begin arm band exercises. Then, if no plyo wall is available on-site, pitchers should still perform 3 plyo ball throws while wearing the TAP Baseball Training Sock: (1) Reverse Throws, (2) Twist and Throws, and (3) Hip Finishers (Table 6.3). These activities are performed by placing the 7 oz plyo ball inside the Training Sock and securing it around the wrist and forearm. The plyo ball is gripped and released inside the sock, just like normal, with each repetition. These exercises are great for warming up the muscles tasked with both acceleration and deceleration of the arm. After completing these plyo ball activities, pitchers can then start throwing standard baseballs with their teammates.

In the same capacity, if the cooldown at a team practice is limited, pitchers should perform our program's cooldown exercises at the conclusion of practice, or at home later that same evening, with no exceptions! Being consistent with all these activities is critical for in-season arm health.

Table 6.3

DEVELOPING A PITCHER
After the Season

Contrary to the opinions of some "experts," we do not advocate for non-injured youth or high school pitchers to take 3-4 months off from overhead throwing at the conclusion of the season, or for that matter, at any other point during the year. One of the greatest mistakes made from an arm care perspective is to initiate strength training of the entire body in the off-season without continuing to throw and perform routine arm care at the same time. These components must be done in conjunction with each other so that arm and shoulder flexibility can further be developed (or maintained) while strength is being built.

An extended period of shoulder inactivity for non-injured pitchers has never been proven to be an optimal strategy for either player development or injury prevention. Surveys from our own players, and even the instructors of our year-round *Arm Care & Velo Program*, show that **arms feel their best when players are more consistently throwing and doing arm care routines**.

Furthermore, studies looking at the timing of the most serious arm injuries afflicting pitchers show an uptick of these injuries occurring during the *early* baseball season.[2] Many hypotheses exist, but one that has <u>not</u> been proposed to explain this phenomenon is: *arms are just way too prepared* for the forces they will see at the start of the season. In fact, usually the opposite is true. Generally speaking, you can't become prepared for anything *if you don't get started preparing*. Promoting extended periods of arm and shoulder atrophy is only counterproductive to this goal.

It is our belief that if your desire is to be an elite mountain climber in treacherous conditions at some point later this year, you will not best prepare yourself for such moments by sitting in a chair. While that statement may be an unfair characterization of the counter argument—since no one is suggesting that pitchers should sit completely idle in chairs for several months—the basic truth still remains: *you will not save the arm by neglecting it.*

. . . .

2 Carr, J. B. 2nd, et al. "Seasonal and monthly trends in elbow ulnar collateral ligament injuries and surgeries: a national epidemiological study." JSES reviews, reports, and techniques vol. 2,1 107-112.

The opinions of some people that do recommend refraining from overhead throwing for large segments of the year arise primarily from misconstruing the observation that kids that play baseball year-round are more likely to have arm injuries. Although that statement is true, it is not true because those kids are doing too much arm care and year-round throwing programs. It is true because *they are not doing enough of them*, mainly because they are playing in too many games, which we've already outlined has potential negative implications on a player's training routines and consistent arm care schedules.

In summary, if the goal of a non-injured pitcher is to continue development and reduce likelihood of future injury, in-season routines should transition into off-season routines without an excessively prolonged after-season delay. We always tell our athletes to take whatever brief vacation time they require at transitional periods, and then get back to being athletes!

Rest & Recovery

While taking 3-4 months off from overhead throwing may be a poor overall strategy for arm health, this does not mean that rest and recovery are not cornerstones of a pitcher's training. To the contrary, they are critical components that must be done routinely throughout the year, and not all at once in a 3-4 month block.

After every high-intensity throwing session year-round, we recommend that our pitchers recover their arms and shoulders with a 30-60 minute session using the Marc Pro (Figure 6.3). In our own practice, the device has now completely replaced the (scientifically questionable) tradition of icing non-injured arms after standard training loads. Excessively cooling areas of the body (e.g., icing) actually *impairs the delivery* of arterial blood that is being sent by the body to enhance recovery. The Marc Pro does the exact opposite.

By using low-frequency electrical impulses, the Marc Pro gently contracts and relaxes muscles without further inducing fatigue. The result is increased circulation for more rapid nutrient delivery post-workout and removal of the metabolic waste generated during the training session. The underlying goal is for our pitchers to recover faster and thus feel better at the time of their next scheduled workout.

While this device does require an investment (given its cost), its quick setup makes it easy to apply in the evenings after workouts when an athlete is resting or finishing up homework. We recommend it to be used for post-workout recovery in any athlete who participates year-round in arm care, strength training, and other sports performance programs.

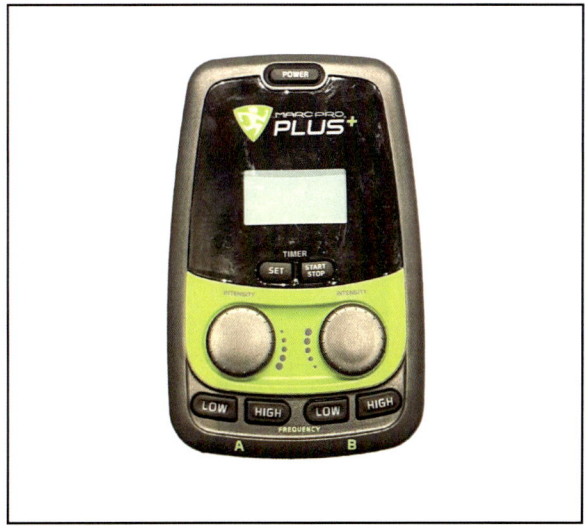

Figure 6.3 - Marc Pro (Recovery)

7
Bullpen Pitching

> "
> I will prepare and some day my chance will come.
> —Abraham Lincoln

The number of innings you get at the youth and high school level to develop as a pitcher will predominantly be determined by a single variable: your ability to throw strikes. If you can learn to do this, you will log more innings and get more time on the mound than your peers. If you fail to do so, you will be replaced in the game. It's as simple as that.

Throwing *one* pitch-type (e.g., fastball) for a strike on a consistent basis is not an easy task. It requires a number of factors to all come together and be executed in a given moment. To have command, a pitcher will need to have *just enough* arm strength, balance, and consistency in stride length and release point on *most* pitches. Each outing will present unique challenges for the pitcher, from opposing hitters, to specific game situations, and even mound conditions. A good pitcher will be someone who can mentally focus and adapt to changing environments.

Throwing *multiple* pitch-types (e.g., fastball, changeup, curveball, and slider) consistently for strikes borders on being nearly impossible for youth or even high school pitchers. It is *that* hard. Each pitch-type has a slightly different grip, release, and finish with the wrist and forearm. The mechanics have to be practiced over and over, typically in a controlled environment at first, before they will translate into pitching success in games. *Bullpen Pitching* is where this skill set gets developed.

Pitch-Type & Grip

A common misconception at most amateur levels is that a particular pitch-type (e.g., curveball) must be thrown with the same standard grip for every pitcher. To the contrary, more than one grip should be experimented with by a given player for each pitch-type, until the most comfortable and effective grip is established for the player's hand size, arm slot, and other mechanical aspects of delivery.

While the typical youth pitcher may not always have access to the (spin-rate measuring) technology that we utilize for instructing our pitchers, the effectiveness of one grip over another for a particular pitch-type can still be observed. One goal of the instructor is to recognize what appears to be working best for each player naturally, and then develop it more.

A few common grips to experiment with by pitch-type are outlined in this chapter, along with pitching instructions and coaching cues. We recommend that pitchers begin experimenting with new grips and pitches during *Flat-Ground Pitching*, before adding them into *Bullpen Pitching* practices. All of this will be discussed in detail later in the chapter.

FASTBALL

GRIPS (Right Hand Displayed)

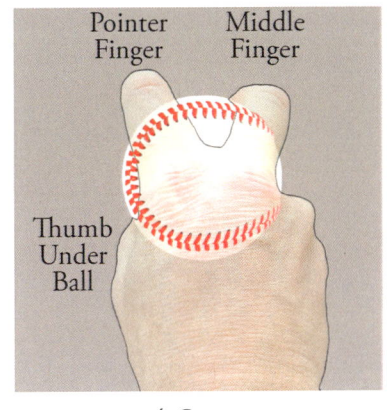
4-Seam

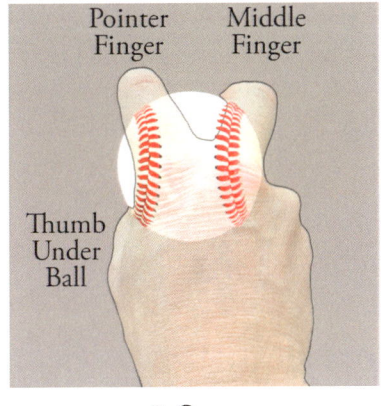
2-Seam

Scan for 360° Visual of Fastball Grips

FASTBALL INSTRUCTION

The fastball is thrown with the pointer and middle fingers *behind* the ball. The elbow fully extends as the ball leaves the hand. A player should think about driving the throwing shoulder "through" (and toward) the catcher's mitt.

COACHING CUES

- "Throw it with your fingers behind the ball."
- "Full elbow extension."
- "Drive your shoulder through the catcher's mitt."
- "Finish out in front."

DEVELOPING A PITCHER

CHANGEUP

GRIPS (Right Hand Displayed)

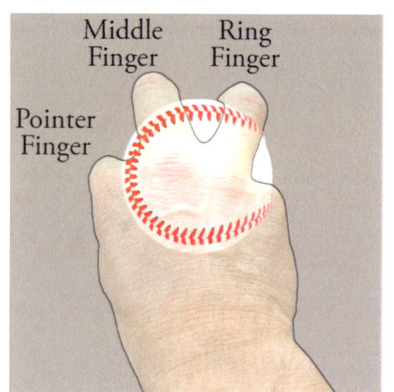
4-Seam

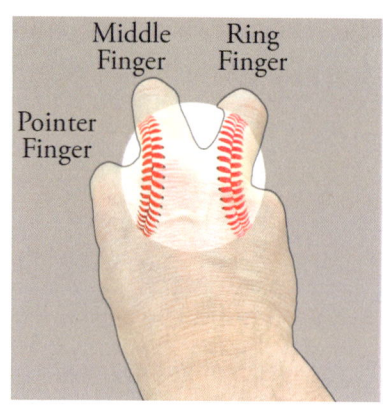
2-Seam

Scan for 360° Visual of Changeup Grips

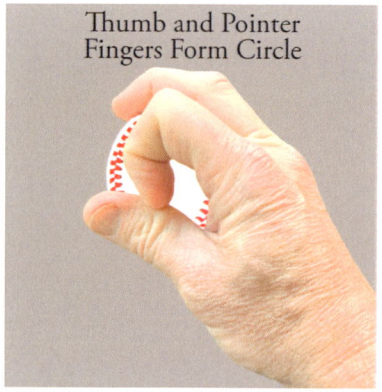
Circle*

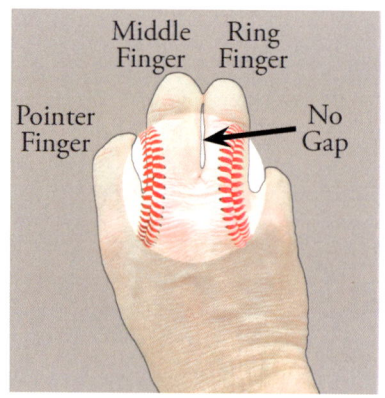
Buddy Fingers*

*The *Circle* and *Buddy Fingers* grips may be incorporated with any grip or ball orientation (e.g., *4-Seam* or *2-Seam*). The defining characteristic of the *Circle* grip is having the thumb and pointer finger form a "circle" on the side of the ball. The defining characteristic of the *Buddy Fingers* grip is having as little of a gap as possible between the middle and ring fingers.

CHANGEUP INSTRUCTION

The changeup (similar to the fastball) is released with two fingers *behind* the ball, but in the case of the changeup, the two fingers are the middle and ring fingers. Arm speed must be maintained and is identical to the fastball. **Do not slow the arm down**. The slower speed of the changeup, relative to the fastball, is not due to a slower arm speed, but instead results from (1) different grip, and (2) more wrist pronation (counter-clockwise rotation of the forearm) on release.

COACHING CUES

- "Roll the fingers over the top of the ball."
- "Pronate the wrist."
- "Swipe the back of the hand to the inside of the ball."
- "Pull the thumb down."

72

CURVEBALL

GRIPS (Right Hand Displayed)

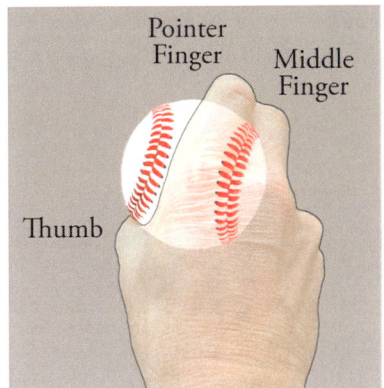
Standard

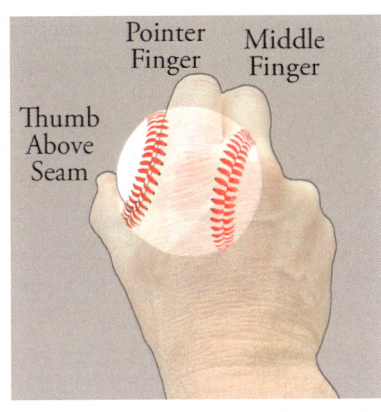
Standard w/ Thumb High

Scan for 360° Visual of Curveball Grips

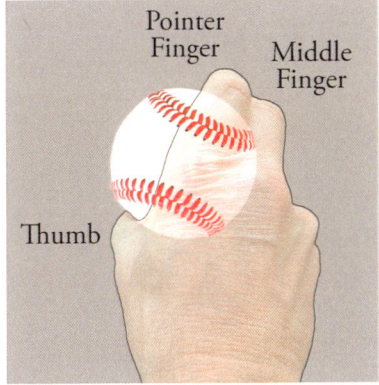
Horseshoe

Spike*

*The *Spike* grip may be incorporated with any grip or ball orientation (e.g., *Standard*, *Standard w/ Thumb High*, or *Horseshoe*). The defining characteristic of the *Spike* grip is a bent pointer finger with only its tip (or fingernail) touching the ball.

CURVEBALL INSTRUCTION

The curveball (unlike the fastball, where two fingers are *behind* the ball) is released with the pointer and middle fingers on the *side* of the ball. Upon release, the wrist undergoes supination (clockwise rotation of the forearm), resulting in the thumb finishing above (or "higher than") the pointer and middle fingers. After the ball leaves the hand, the elbow remains bent and not fully extended ("short-arm" finish). The arm and forearm move in a "chopping" motion down and into the opposite rib cage.

COACHING CUES

- "Fingers on the side of the ball."
- "Short-arm finish."
- "Pull your hand into your opposite rib cage."
- "Try to chop the belly button."
- "Roll the thumb over the top of the ball."
- "Throw it with the back of your hand."

DEVELOPING A PITCHER

SLIDER

GRIPS (Right Hand Displayed)

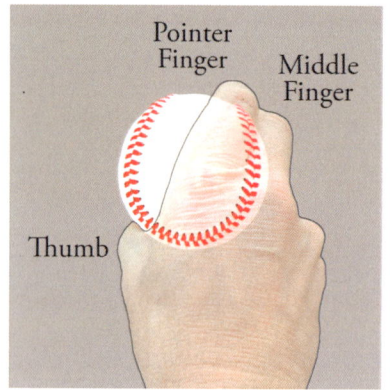
Standard Low-Set

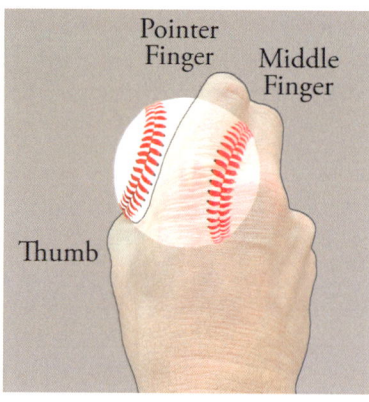
Standard High-Set

Scan for 360° Visual of Slider Grips

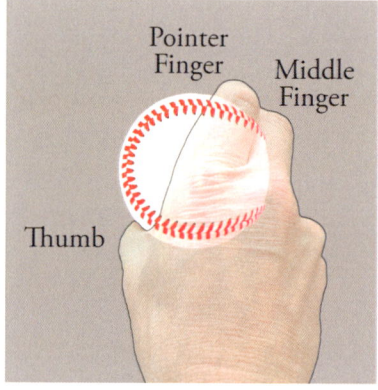
4-Seam Offset

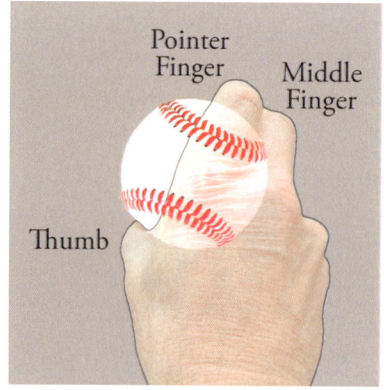
Horseshoe

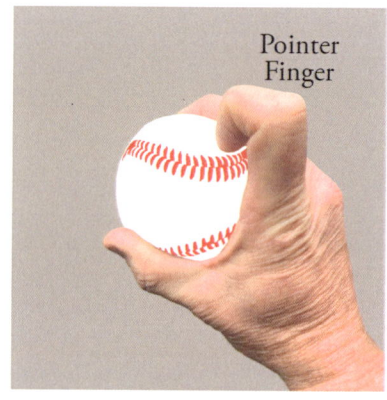
Spike*

*The *Spike* grip may be used with any of the grips that are shown.

SLIDER INSTRUCTION

The slider (similar to the curveball) is released with the <u>pointer</u> and <u>middle fingers</u> on the *side* of the ball. Unlike the curveball (where the wrist supinates), the wrist pronates (counter-clockwise rotation) on release of the slider. This enables the two fingers on the side of the ball to "slash" inward, cutting through the bottom of the ball as the thumb is driven downward. The overall wrist motion is nearly identical to what is required to throw a spiral with a football. Similar to the fastball, the elbow will also extend.

COACHING CUES

- "Fingers on the side of the ball."
- "Slash the bottom of the ball."
- "Roll the back of the pointer finger under the ball."
- "Throw it like a football."

Flat-Ground Pitching

Flat-Ground Pitching is defined as the practice of pitching (from either the windup or stretch) on flat ground, typically at **shorter pitching distances**, and usually at sub-maximal intensity levels (~90%). For example, if a high school pitcher normally throws off the mound at 60.5 ft from home plate, *Flat-Ground Pitching* is performed at a distance of about 50-55 ft with no mound involved. For a youth pitcher who normally throws at a distance of 46 ft from home plate, *Flat-Ground Pitching* is performed at a distance of about 38-42 ft with no mound involved.

Flat-Ground Pitching enables the pitcher to primarily focus on the grip and release of each pitch-type. Relative to throwing off the mound, it puts less strain on the arm and the shoulder, so many pitches can be thrown in this setting. We use this activity to get more repetitions when practicing new pitch-types and/or grips.

At any point in the year—whether it be the off-season or the in-season—when a pitcher needs more recovery time between bullpens, we simply replace a scheduled *Bullpen Pitching* day with a *Flat-Ground Pitching* day. This enables a pitcher to still practice various pitch-types without over-training the arm.

Bullpen Pitch Count & Weekly Frequency

The pitch count for a bullpen day must be individualized, taking into account player age, arm velocity, season of the year, and proximity of the day to any upcoming games (in-season). The following tables are intended as a general guide for the average pitcher and can be easily adapted:

Off-Season	
Pitches Per Bullpen	40 to 60
Frequency	1 day / week

<u>Notes:</u> Because multiple days per week during the off-season are being devoted to high-intensity throwing as part of the *Arm Care & Velo Program*, the main purpose of a bullpen this time of year is to maintain muscle memory of the release point as the body is changing (i.e., gaining in overall strength and arm velocity). New grips and pitch-types are also best experimented with at this time.

Pre-Season	
Pitches Per Bullpen	50 to 70
Frequency	2 days / week

<u>Notes:</u> With the body stronger and the arm well-conditioned from off-season work, the preseason ramp-up time is mainly used to improve control of a pitcher's two (or three) best pitch-types. If pitchers begin the season too wild on the mound, they lose early season opportunities to work themselves into a pitching rotation. For this reason, we increase the frequency of bullpens in the preseason to twice weekly. In early preseason, total pitch count per session can start at about 40 pitches, and then slowly be titrated upward each week to the recommended range given above. Do not forget that the preseason is predominantly the time to achieve control of existing pitch-types, and not to begin experimenting with something new.

DEVELOPING A PITCHER

In-Season	
Pitches Per Bullpen	Variable* (usually 30 to 65) *Highly dependent on pitches already thrown (or anticipated to be thrown) in games during the week.
Frequency	2 days / week (counting games and bullpens)

<u>Notes:</u> Pitchers should throw off the mound a minimum of 2 days per week during the season, whether that be in a game, at a team practice, or on their own time. This does not mean that every bullpen needs to be lengthy, especially when a player is already throwing on other days of the week. It does mean, however, that a routine must be performed consistently, or pitch command for a pitcher will be hard to find upon entering games. Players should understand bullpens under 30 pitches are typically not too fatiguing for the arm and may be performed even up to 48 hours prior to a scheduled game. This means for a standard high school baseball season with games on Tuesdays and Fridays, if a player doesn't pitch on Tuesday, the player can throw a bullpen (up to 30 pitches) on Wednesday, and still pitch in Friday's game. Likewise, if a pitcher does not pitch on Friday, the player can throw a bullpen over the weekend, and still be ready to pitch the following Tuesday.

Bullpen Routine

More than one bullpen format has been implemented and found to be effective for a pitcher, but we will share our standard approach, by competition level, to give you some guidance.

All Levels

For every pitcher, as explained in Chapter 6, we follow the *Arm Care & Velo Program* modified for bullpen pitching days (p. 63). This includes the warm-up, some plyo ball throws, and Whip Behinds, followed by the bullpen session and cooldown. *Bullpen Pitching* (or *Flat-Ground Pitching* when substituted) generally consists of throwing each pitch-type consecutively for a group of pitches, followed by cycling through each pitch-type, one at a time, for the remainder of the session.

The Beginner Level

At the beginner level, the entire bullpen is usually ONE pitch-type, the fastball. If a fastball cannot be thrown consistently near the strike zone yet, there is no reason to do anything else. We usually have the pitcher throw 10 fastballs with the 4-seam grip, followed by 10 fastballs with the 2-seam grip. Then, we alternate the 4-seam grip with the 2-seam grip, every other pitch, for the remainder of the bullpen. A large part of a pitcher's early development is learning to be comfortable with changing pitch grips, and we train this skill set from the onset with the fastball.

After every 5 bullpen pitches, we have our pitchers change from the *4-Step Windup* to the stretch position, even if they are not required to do so in their Little League yet. Training both the windup and the stretch position at a younger age has a number of obvious benefits, but we do it mainly because it fits with our philosophy: "When pitchers get comfortable, introduce change, and force them to adapt to something different."

Intermediate Level

Once a pitcher has established *enough* control with the fastball, we add additional pitch-types to the routine. We typically define *enough* control at this stage as the ability to throw 3 or more strikes out of 5 pitches in at least 2 of 4 sets—or, more generally speaking, **a strike percentage greater than 50%**.

When *enough* control exists with a fastball of any grip, the next pitch-type we add is the changeup. At this level, the pitcher usually begins the bullpen by throwing 10 fastballs, followed by 10 changeups. In the early stages of learning a new pitch-type, we may instruct an alternate grip to the player, or provide different coaching cues, about every 3-5 pitches. After throwing the first set of 10 changeups, we usually add a second set of 10 changeups, especially if it is obvious that the new pitch-type will require more repetitions.

After 30 total pitches, we alternate the fastball with the changeup, every other pitch, for the remainder of the bullpen, ultimately gravitating to the grips that appear to be the most successful (or comfortable) for that player. Periodically, we pause the session to review the player's grip, and reiterate any coaching cues for the pitch-type being thrown. We alternate throwing from the windup and the stretch every 5 bullpen pitches.

Advanced Level

When *enough* control has been achieved with TWO pitch-types (fastball and changeup), the next pitch-type we add is the curveball. Age-appropriate concerns related to the timing of when to introduce a curveball will be discussed at the end of this chapter, but once a curveball has been added, the bullpen begins as follows: 10 fastballs, 10 changeups, 10 curveballs. In the early stages of learning the curveball, we may introduce an

DEVELOPING A PITCHER

alternate grip to the player, or provide different coaching cues, about every 3-5 pitches. After throwing the first set of 10 curveballs, we usually add a second set of 10 curveballs, especially if it is obvious that the new pitch-type will require more repetitions.

After 40 total pitches, we rotate through all three pitch-types in sets for the remainder of the bullpen, ultimately gravitating to the grips that appear to be the most successful (or comfortable) for that player. Periodically, we pause the session to review the player's grip, and reiterate any coaching cues for the pitch-type being thrown. We alternate throwing from the windup and the stretch every 5 bullpen pitches.

Once a player has gained adequate experience with three pitch-types, the bullpen simply becomes a routine of 10 fastballs, 10 changeups, and 10 curveballs, followed by rotating through all three pitch-types in sets for the remainder of the session (Table 7.1).

When only 30 total pitches are scheduled for a bullpen, we modify the start to be 5 fastballs, 5 changeups, and 5 curveballs, so that rotating through the pitch-types after every pitch can still be performed in the latter half of the session.

For any given pitcher, other pitch-types (e.g., slider, cutter, etc.) can obviously be added to, or substituted for any of the previously mentioned

Bullpen Routine (3 Pitch-Types)

Set Number	Pitch-Type	Pitches	Windup/Stretch Pitch Breakdown
1	Fastball	10*	Windup (5) Stretch (5)
2	Changeup	10*	Windup (5) Stretch (5)
3	Curveball (or Slider)	10*	Windup (5) Stretch (5)
	*If only 30 total pitches are scheduled to be thrown, decrease to 5		
4	Fastball	1	Windup (3)
4	Changeup	1	Windup (3)
4	Curveball (or Slider)	1	Windup (3)
5	Fastball	1	Stretch (3)
5	Changeup	1	Stretch (3)
5	Curveball (or Slider)	1	Stretch (3)
6+	Repeat Sets #4 and #5 until bullpen pitch count is reached, adjusting targeted pitch location (e.g., inside, outside, high, low) with each new set.		

Table 7.1

pitch-types. No matter how many different pitch-types are thrown in the bullpen, the routine remains consistent, with each pitch-type thrown consecutively for a set number of pitches, followed by rotating through all of the pitch-types in sets for the remainder of the session. The targeting of pitch locations (e.g., inside, outside, high, and low) is incorporated into the later sets at the more advanced levels, as pitchers gain increasing confidence in their control.

Additional Comments About Pitch-Types

We tell our youth and high school pitchers that on any given day, they really **just need command of TWO pitch-types to be successful**. That is the reason why our standard approach to *Bullpen Pitching* is to focus on throwing, and thus developing THREE pitch-types during every session. At the competition levels that we have mentioned, it is rare for pitchers to have command of *every* single pitch in their arsenal *every* single game, so by learning THREE pitch-types well, it increases the likelihood that at least TWO of them will be *good enough*, on a given day.

There is no specific rule that requires the THREE pitch-types selected to be a fastball, changeup, and curveball. There is also no rule that says a fourth (or fifth) pitch-type cannot be developed either. As examples, many of our high school athletes throw their bullpens with the following three pitch-types: fastball, changeup, and slider (no curveball). Some have a cutter (or a splitter) as an additional pitch-type. All of this must be individualized by pitcher in order to take advantage of any particular strengths recognized.

One main point of emphasis is **to refrain from adding more pitch-types until enough control is obtained with existing ones**. The majority of youth and high school pitchers may never progress beyond throwing three pitch-types, and that is fine. We will say it again: it is always better to throw two pitch-types well, with command, than four pitch-types poorly.

What's the Ideal Age for Curveballs?

The age-old comment that "you should not throw a curveball until your teenage years, because it will hurt your arm," is not rooted in any scientific analysis of kinematic sequences or actual measurements of torque on the elbow. It previously arose from "expert" opinion alone, and such "experts" were circulating and passing down these recommendations long before the technology even existed to quantitatively measure the forces involved in throwing.

In more recent years, technological advances have enabled us to better study whether or not a curveball truly puts more strain on a pitcher's arm, and the results have been overwhelmingly consistent: **curveballs do NOT produce higher stress loads on the throwing shoulder and elbow**. The study of kinematic data on teenage pitchers has actually found forces on the shoulder and elbow to be LESS with curveballs than fastballs.[1] Biomechanical study of youth pitchers

---

1 Nissen, C.W., et al. "A biomechanical comparison of the fastball and curveball in adolescent baseball pitchers." *The American Journal of Sports Medicine* vol. 37,8 (2009): 1492-8.

DEVELOPING A PITCHER

utilizing 3D motion analysis has come to an identical conclusion, finding that fastballs (in comparison to curveballs and changeups) produce the greatest proximal forces at the shoulder and the elbow, the greatest varus torque at the elbow, and the greatest shoulder internal rotation torque.[2] Studies using different modalities, such as the Motus mTHROW Sleeve, to examine forces on the arm, have produced similar results, again showing that fastballs typically generate the highest amount of elbow torque and are the most stressful pitch on the arm when compared to curveballs and changeups.[3]

Even observational studies (which retrospectively seek to evaluate the past "habits" of injured pitchers compared to controls) have largely been unable to associate increased arm pain with curveballs.[4] A study of 481 youth pitchers did not find throwing a curveball prior to age 13 to be a significant risk factor for serious arm injury.[5] Cadaver studies assessing strain with valgus loading on the anterior and posterior bundles of the elbow's ulnar collateral ligament (UCL) have also contradicted the assertion that forearm supination, which is seen with the curveball pitch-type, elevates the risk of injury.[6]

> **In more recent years, technological advances have enabled us to better study whether or not a curveball truly puts more strain on a pitcher's arm, and the results have been overwhelmingly consistent: curveballs do NOT produce higher stress loads on the throwing shoulder and elbow.**

---

[2] Dun, Shouchen, et al. "A biomechanical comparison of youth baseball pitches: is the curveball potentially harmful?." The American Journal of Sports Medicine vol. 36,4 (2008): 686-92.

[3] Gielen, and Astrid. "Fastballs vs. Offspeed Pitches - Comparative and Relative Elbow Stress." Driveline Baseball, 3 May 2022, https://www.drivelinebaseball.com/2017/02/fastballs-offspeed-pitches-comparative-relative-elbow-stress/?srsltid=AfmBOoqodIl54LQ0SUJyMt-bMNbtbM-S8lpBga87c3NBtPr3BMEDlV-n. Accessed 5/4/2025.

[4] Olsen, S. J. 2nd, et al. "Risk factors for shoulder and elbow injuries in adolescent baseball pitchers." The American Journal of Sports Medicine vol. 34,6 (2006): 905-12.

[5] Fleisig, G. S., et al. "Risk of serious injury for young baseball pitchers: a 10-year prospective study." The American Journal of Sports Medicine vol. 39,2 (2011): 253-7.

[6] Pribyl, C. R., et al. "Elbow ligament strain under valgus load: a biomechanical study." Orthopedics vol. 22,6 (1999): 607-12.

In conclusion, multiple systemic reviews, compiling the results of over a dozen biomechanical and epidemiological studies, do not support that curveballs have an increased risk of injury compared to fastballs.[7] We feel that one review by Tamate and Garber[8] sums it up best:

> "Longstanding taboos against teaching curveballs to pitchers before puberty remains ingrained in youth baseball. This is despite a deficiency of convincing evidence in both biomechanical and epidemiological research showing increased harm. Larger studies with improved control of confounding variables may eventually reveal curveballs to be the dangerous pitch that many believe it to be. However, at present, the sports medicine community has no good evidence to recommend against its use."

For all these reasons, we do not place a specific limitation on what age players must be before they can be taught how to appropriately throw a curveball. Most youth will attempt to throw them on their own at early ages anyway, and we would prefer to be a part of the process of instructing them correctly. In our experience, when you can throw a fastball and a changeup for *enough* strikes in the bullpen, you are ready to learn how to throw a curveball.

---

[7] *Grantham, W. J., et al. "The curveball as a risk factor for injury: a systematic review." Sports Health vol. 7,1 (2015): 19-26.*

[8] *Tamate, T. M., and Garber, A. C. "Curveballs in Youth Pitchers: A Review of the Current Literature." Hawai'i Journal of Health & Social Welfare vol. 78,11 Suppl 2 (2019): 16-20.*

8
Strength Program

> "
> We are what we repeatedly do. Excellence then, is not an act, but a habit.
> —Aristotle

If you get the opportunity to make the trip to Omaha, Nebraska, this coming June, the current site of college baseball's College World Series each year, you will be hard-pressed to witness a pitcher who does not appear to be very strong. You will watch pitch after pitch being delivered by powerful thighs driving forcefully down the mound. It has become the norm, and that's because *strength matters*. If one team has players with all the intangibles, and another, the exact same players, but physically stronger, it's the second team that wins.

Sport-specific training, or what more recently has been termed *functional training*, got its start for good reason. It was not too many generations ago that the entire practice for high school

DEVELOPING A PITCHER

pitchers (on non-pitching days) just involved jogging back-and-forth between the foul poles, as if pitchers were training to be cross-country runners. The basis for this was that a pitcher needed to be "in shape," in order to throw for hours or more in a game. Of course, what was completely being overlooked was the *actual scope of work* that pitchers were having to perform during these games.

Pitchers need to be explosive for just a moment's time in order to deliver pitches at breakneck speeds. Then, they need to pause, rest for twenty seconds or so, and be explosive again. Pitchers repeat this activity for about 15 repetitions in an inning, sometimes more, sometimes less, and then head back to the dugout, where they usually will sit down. Very little about jogging foul pole to foul pole is really helping them prepare for this activity. Such training is just not *functional*.

The benefits gained through more sport-specific training, however, quickly erode when attempts are made to make *all* strength and performance training *functional*. An overemphasis on these functional components in the weight room becomes a detriment to the athlete when the trainer fails to grasp strength's primary role in sports and how it's most efficiently acquired.

As an example, swinging a baseball bat requires coordinated movements of the forearms, arms, shoulders, back, abdomen, and legs. For simplicity, the upper body motion alone involves the deltoids, biceps, triceps, pectoralis major, and latissimus dorsi. It would be a fallacy to suggest the best way to acquire strength in all of these muscles is by *functionally* swinging a club weighing ounces (or even pounds) around the torso.

Others before us have used a similar analogy,[1] but it deserves to be repeated here: just because a cyclist's hamstring is never flexed beyond 90 degrees on a bike, does not mean that a cyclist's hamstring is best trained by performing partial squats. To the contrary, a partial squat (in comparison to a full-depth squat) develops a less powerful hamstring contraction, which is obviously less desirable for competitive cyclists.

....

1 *Rippetoe M., and Baker, A. Practical Programming for Strength Training. 3rd Edition, Wichita Falls, Texas, The Aasgaard Company, 2013.*

STRENGTH TRAINING | 8

In summary, our approach to strength and performance training is characterized by the following concept: strength is built *best* when the *best* exercises to build strength are being done. In most cases, this means strength is better developed at the youth and high school levels outside of sport-specific movements. Strength is best achieved in non-specific ways through fundamental exercises that enable you to lift increasingly heavier weights over longer ranges of motion—like the Squat, Bench Press, and Press. Whenever strength is gained and flexibility is maintained, the result is a *more functional* muscle for sport-specific activities.

Although the above concept is foundational to our approach, it should not be taken out of context to mean that a pitcher should *never* jog. In fact, if training were to only consist of either *sitting* or *jogging*, our bias would be to strongly encourage endurance running—if for no other reason than it elevates core body temperature, temporarily increases cardiac output, helps maintain joint mobility, and even promotes mental health by reducing stress and improving mood and cognitive function.[2]

But jogging, like other functional exercises of limited resistance in the weight room, cannot be the sole basis of a pitcher's strength and conditioning program. These things are merely additions to it. The foundation of a good strength program for a pitcher is one that gets you the strongest in the least amount of time without compromising safety, so that more time is available on a routine basis to perform the *functional* (throwing and pitching) activities outlined in prior chapters.

. . . .

[2] *Oswald, Freya, et al. "A Scoping Review of the Relationship between Running and Mental Health." International Journal of Environmental Research and Public Health vol. 17,21 (1 Nov 2020): 8059.*

DEVELOPING A PITCHER

The Early Years: Bodyweight Training (Generally Under Age 12)

The youth's body is consistently growing and must first become accustomed to itself before any additional weight or resistance is added. *Moving well* requires balance and coordinated muscular efforts between the upper and lower body transmitted through the core. Since balance, by itself, is also directly proportional to strength, the formula for moving well can best be thought of in the following manner, with strength essentially counting <u>twice</u>:

$$\text{Moving Well} = \text{Balance} \times (\text{Strength})^2$$

The process for building strength in *The Early Years* (typically under age 12) begins with the performance of bodyweight exercises. The main purpose at this younger stage is to learn a few of the non-specific movement patterns that will later be used to most efficiently build strength in the adolescent years. The other key goal at this point is merely to establish an early habit of strength training on a consistent basis throughout the entire year. As we like to say: "Begin by doing small things well, and then keep doing them, over and over again."

Basic bodyweight training in *The Early Years* consists of learning 6 exercises, with many of them being ones in which you are likely already familiar:

- Squats
- Push-Ups
- Sit-Ups
- Bulgarian Split Squats
- Single-Leg Glute Bridges
- Ball Pick-Ups

We will outline each of the 6 exercises first, and then provide a sample weekly schedule showing how they can be integrated into a routine.

> "
> **Moving well equals balance times strength squared, with strength essentially counting <u>twice</u>.**

STRENGTH TRAINING | 8

SQUATS

EXPLAINED: (A) Feet position will vary slightly based upon player anatomy, but a good starting point for most players will be with the heels shoulder-width apart and toes pointed out at about a 30° angle. (B) Shove the knees out while going down, so that the knees finish over the toes, but not beyond them. The two most common mistakes made with the knees are: (1) buckling the knees inward (instead of SHOVING them outward), and (2) allowing the knees to come too far forward (past the toes) on the way down. (C) Once the knees reach a position directly above the toes, continue to *sit the bottom down and back* until it reaches one inch below parallel (relative to the knees). At that point, drive the bottom directly UPWARD (not forward) and return to the starting position. The neck should remain relaxed and not crane upward during the squat, with eye gaze being toward the floor about 5 ft in front of the player.

Scan for Visual

A.

Starting Position
Heels shoulder-width apart and toes pointed out at about 30°

B.

Front View

SHOVE the knees outward and finish over the toes.

C.

Side View

1" below parallel

Keep the knees from drifting beyond the toes.

DEVELOPING A PITCHER

PUSH-UPS

EXPLAINED: (A) With the legs and elbows fully extended and toes touching the ground, place both palms on the ground slightly wider than shoulder-width apart. (B) Keep the back straight and in-line with the hips, while bending the elbows, until the chest comes in contact with the blue foam pad. Push back up to the starting position.

Scan for Visual

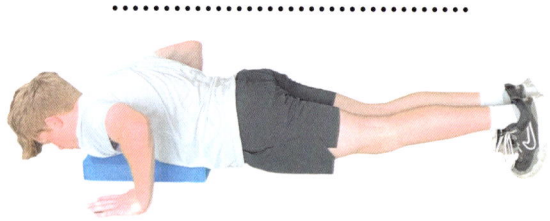

A.   B.

SIT-UPS

EXPLAINED: (A) Lie on the back with knees bent and both feet flat on the ground (either fixed in place by a partner, or safely underneath an object to secure them). (B) Cross the arms to the chest and contract the abdominal muscles in order to bring the chest to the knees. Return back to the starting position. (Note: A Rogue Wise Crack AbMat, from RogueFitness.com, is shown beneath the athlete, and adds stability and tailbone protection.)

Scan for Visual

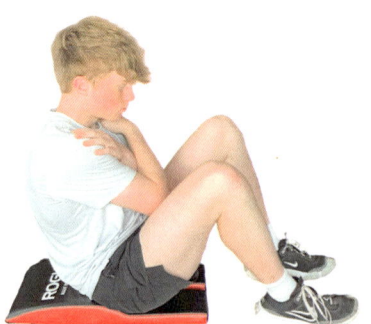

A.   B.

STRENGTH TRAINING | 8

BULGARIAN SPLIT SQUATS

EXPLAINED: (A) Stand on the left leg and place the dorsal side of the right foot on a chair or bench. (B) Bend the left leg until the right knee is a couple inches from the floor. Return to the starting position by thinking about *driving the left heel into the floor*. Complete all repetitions with the left leg. Then, reverse leg positions, and perform the same number of repetitions with the right leg.

Scan for Visual

A.

B.

SINGLE-LEG GLUTE BRIDGES

EXPLAINED: (A) Lie on the back with the right leg straight and the left leg bent at the knee. (B) Keeping the left foot fixed on the ground, raise the right leg and buttocks off the floor, until the chest, abdomen, and both thighs are in-line with each other. Hold for 1 second and return to the floor. Complete the assigned repetitions raising the right leg off the floor, and then reverse leg positions, performing the same number of repetitions with the other leg.

Scan for Visual

A.   B.

89

DEVELOPING A PITCHER

BALL PICK-UPS

EXPLAINED: Place a baseball (or similar ball) in front of the right foot. (A) Lift the right knee waist-high to assume the starting position, with only the left foot touching the ground. (B) Bend down and pick up the baseball with the right hand. (C) Lift the ball and right knee back up to the starting position, and then return the ball to the ground. This is one repetition. Complete all assigned repetitions while balancing on the left leg first. Then, reverse leg positions, and perform the same number of repetitions while balancing on the other leg.

Scan for Visual

A. Place the ball out in front of the right foot and lift the right knee.

B. Bend down and pick the ball up with the right hand, while balancing on the left leg.

C. Raise the ball and right knee up, then place the ball back on the ground.

90

Sample Weekly Off-Season Plan for Bodyweight Training

The 6 bodyweight exercises can be implemented in a number of ways throughout *The Early Years*. A sample weekly schedule, specifically the 4th week in a typical 6-week off-season program for a team of 9-year-olds, is provided in the table below. (Note: The first few weeks of this program would have involved less repetitions for each exercise, and the later weeks would have involved more. As youth players become acclimated to their routine and gain strength, repetitions can be added each week. We've found that our youth enjoy using a deck of playing cards to determine repetitions for their exercises, as explained at the bottom of the table.)

Exercise	Mon	Tue	Wed	Thu	Fri	Sat	Sun
Dynamic Warm-up & Static Stretching (See Chapter 2)	Complete Full Routine	Complete Full Routine	X	Complete Full Routine	Complete Full Routine	X	X
Ball Pick-Ups	Goal: 40 Reps ▪2 Sets x 10 (Right Leg) ▪2 Sets x 10 (Left Leg)	X	X	Goal: 40 Reps ▪2 Sets x 10 (Right Leg) ▪2 Sets x 10 (Left Leg)	X	X	X
Bulgarian Split Squats	Goal: 60 Reps ▪3 Sets x 10 (Right Leg) ▪3 Sets x 10 (Left Leg)	X	X	Goal: 60 Reps ▪3 Sets x 10 (Right Leg) ▪3 Sets x 10 (Left Leg)	X	X	X
Squats	Goal: 36 Reps ▪3 Sets x 12	X	X	Goal: 36 Reps ▪3 Sets x 12	X	X	X
Single-Leg Glute Bridges	X	Goal: 60 Reps ▪3 Sets x 10 (Right Leg) ▪3 Sets x 10 (Left Leg)	X	X	Goal: 60 Reps ▪3 Sets x 10 (Right Leg) ▪3 Sets x 10 (Left Leg)	X	X
Push-Ups	X	Goal: 8 Cards*	X	X	Goal: 8 Cards*	X	X
Sit-Ups	X	Goal: 8 Cards*	X	X	Goal: 8 Cards*	X	X
X = OFF DAY FROM ACTIVITY							

*Draw a random card from a deck of standard playing cards and perform the exercise for the number of reps specified on the card. Aces are worth 25 reps, face cards are 10, and numbered cards are their numbers.

DEVELOPING A PITCHER

The Later Years: Resistance Training (Generally Age 12 & Up)

The transition from bodyweight only exercises to resistance (weight) training is traditionally made around age 12, but the ideal time will vary by individual athlete and the resources available. Given our own expertise, we have a high comfort level in introducing weight training at younger ages (e.g., ages 9 and 10). The in-person instruction we provide our youth athletes, however, may not be readily available to everyone, and there is obviously a higher standard to meet for safety when weights are added. That said, resistance training can be safely performed in younger youth, and the data supporting it has been reproduced innumerable times.

One study of young teenagers found only 0.0012 injuries per 100 participant hours in organized weightlifting activities, which was about 5,170 times safer than soccer (6.2 injuries per 100 participant hours).[3] Multiple other studies, with many involving children as young as ages 6 to 10, showed resistance training to be well-tolerated by youth, with injury rates either very low or even zero.[4] Physical education classes at school are apparently twice as dangerous as organized sport activities, and weightlifting consistently has been found to be one of the safest activities within that latter group.[5]

In general, when youth athletes have proven themselves to be coachable and have shown a pattern of discipline and consistency with performing bodyweight exercises, they are ready for resistance training.

....

3 Hamill, B.P. "Relative safety of weightlifting and weight training." Journal of Strength and Conditioning Research. 8,1 (1994):53-57.

4 Faigenbaum, A. D., and Myer, G. D. "Resistance training among young athletes: safety, efficacy and injury prevention effects." British Journal of Sports Medicine vol. 44,1 (2010): 56-63.

5 Zaricznyj, B. et al. "Sports-related injuries in school-aged children." The American Journal of Sports Medicine vol. 8,5 (1980): 318-24.

"

One study of young teenagers found only 0.0012 injuries per 100 participant hours in organized weightlifting activities, which was about 5,170 times safer than soccer.

> **Weight training *consistency* is the variable most influential to achieving strength gains.**

For the complete weight training novice, getting in-person instruction is the best way to learn the correct form for the lifts that will be most efficient at building strength: squat, bench press, and press. However, these lifts can also be self-taught or instructed by well-informed parents. If parents are seeking the necessary knowledge to get started with their own son or daughter, the book, *Starting Strength Basic Barbell Training*,[6] by Rippetoe and colleagues, is indispensable.

Weight training *consistency* is the variable most influential to achieving strength gains, and we strongly encourage developing a time-efficient system that can be performed, at least in some capacity, year-round. In our experience, school weight training programs are generally inconsistent, so dedicated athletes will usually need a separate system in place to complete their routines at various times throughout the year. Monthly memberships at training facilities (like our own), or fitness clubs, are what most players will do, since personal equipment for strength training can be a large investment. That said, we've found that a small squat rack, bench, and barbell at home, if space allows, is often the only way for some athletes to maintain consistency during time-crunched periods of the year. If used by all, this equipment becomes an investment in health for the entire family, too.

In the following pages, you will encounter two general sections: (1) *The Lifts*, which explains the 3 lifts that youth to high school athletes should perform to most efficiently start their development of generalized strength, and (2) the *Accessory Exercises*, which describes 4 additional exercises specific to developing a pitcher's grip and arm strength. The limited coaching tips provided here for each lift and exercise are not meant to be comprehensive, and by themselves, are insufficient to certify any athlete to perform them. We recommend that an instructor with expertise in coaching these lifts and exercises be involved with their initiation to better drive performance and ensure safety.

---

6 *Rippetoe M., and Bradford, S. Starting Strength Basic Barbell Training. 3rd Edition, Wichita Falls, Texas, The Aasgaard Company, 2017.*

DEVELOPING A PITCHER

THE LIFTS: SQUAT

Scan for Visual

EXPLAINED: (A) Using the same squat technique learned from body-weight training, position the heels shoulder-width apart and toes pointed out at about a 30° angle. Position the barbell on the back, just under the spine of the scapula. (B) Shove the knees out while dropping the bottom to a depth of 1" below parallel, at which point the knees should be over the toes. Then, drive the hips/bottom upward.

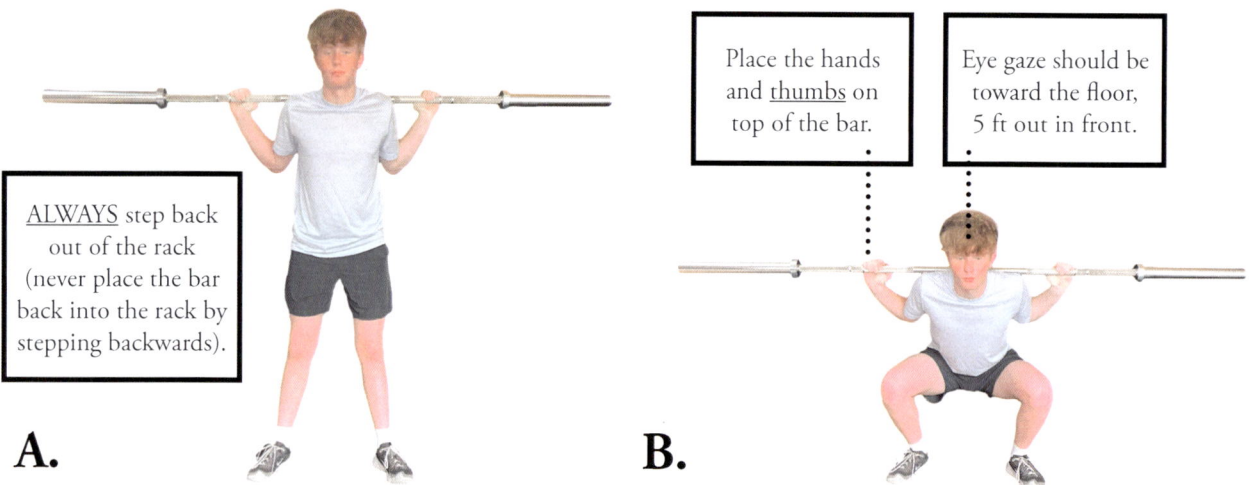

Place the hands and <u>thumbs</u> on top of the bar.

Eye gaze should be toward the floor, 5 ft out in front.

<u>ALWAYS</u> step back out of the rack (never place the bar back into the rack by stepping backwards).

A.

B.

THE LIFTS: BENCH PRESS

Scan for Visual

EXPLAINED: (A) Lie with the bottom and upper back touching the bench, and both feet flat on the ground. Grip the bar wider than shoulder-width apart (usually between 22" to 28"). Resting the bar in the palms, wrap the fingers and thumbs around it. *(Never use a thumb-less grip with any barbell exercise other than the squat.)* Unrack the bar and move it out to the lockout position, directly over the shoulder joints. (B) Lower the bar until it touches the middle of the sternum. Drive it back to the lockout position.

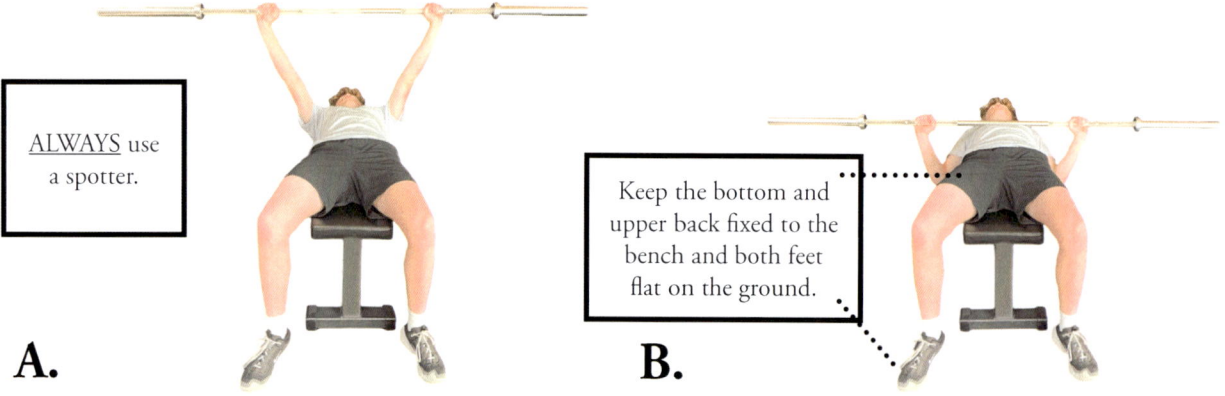

<u>ALWAYS</u> use a spotter.

Keep the bottom and upper back fixed to the bench and both feet flat on the ground.

A.

B.

THE LIFTS: PRESS

EXPLAINED: (A) Wrap the fingers and thumbs around the bar, extend the wrists, and rest the bar in the palms. Unrack the weight and step backwards to assume the starting position. (B) Shove the pelvis forward, *keeping the knees and spine locked*. Then, press the bar upward. As it travels, the pelvis should move backward, finishing directly underneath the bar. (C) Lock the elbows and shrug the shoulders to reach the *lockout position*. Return to the starting position.

Scan for Visual

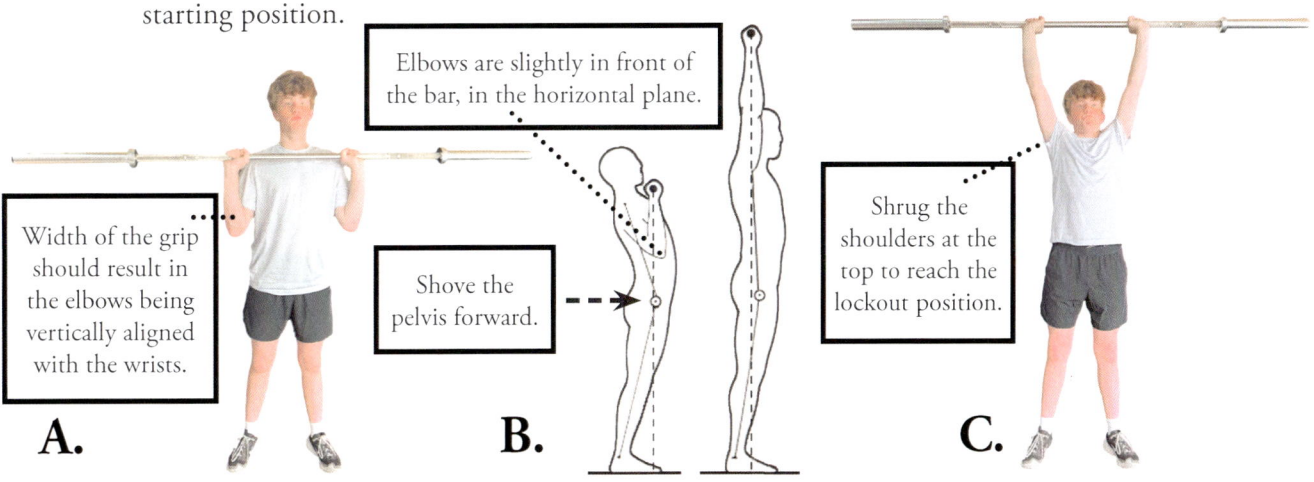

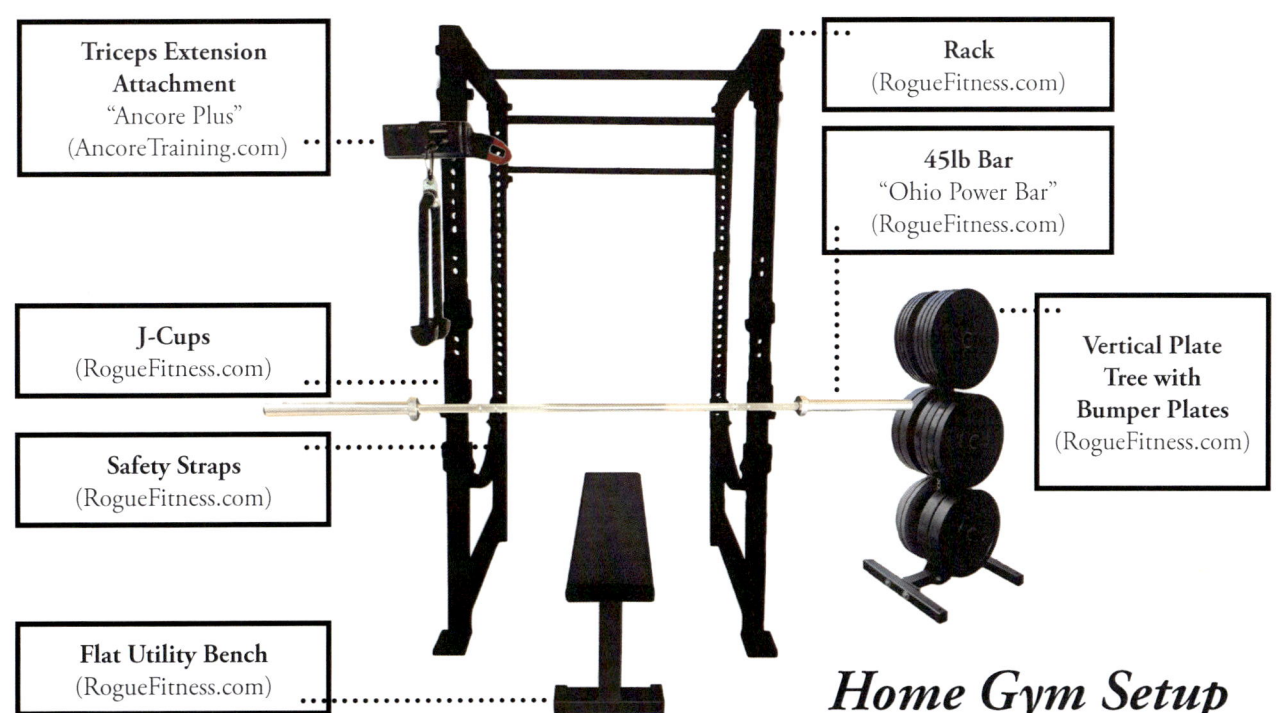

Home Gym Setup

DEVELOPING A PITCHER

ACCESSORY EXERCISES: WRIST CURL

EXPLAINED: (A) In a seated position, grip the bar with the palms facing upward, and place the back of the forearms on top of the thighs. Extend the wrists slightly, allowing the bar to roll down into the tips of the fingers. (B) Then, flex ("curl") the wrists and fingers, while still keeping the back of the forearms fixed on top of the thighs. Return to the starting position.

Scan for Visual

Allow the bar to roll into the fingertips, but do NOT drop the bar on your toes.

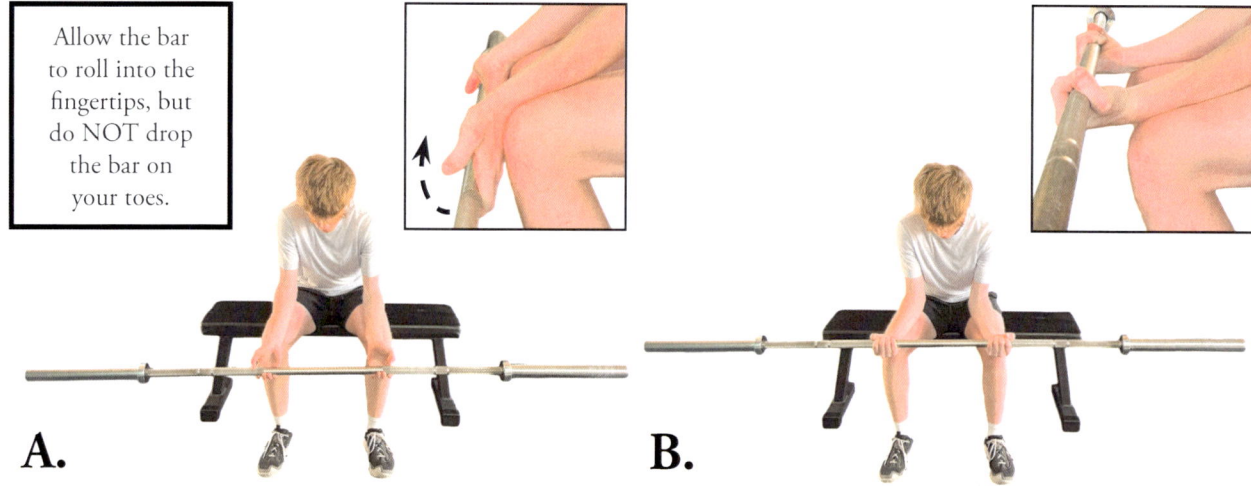

A. B.

ACCESSORY EXERCISES: REVERSE WRIST CURL

EXPLAINED: In a seated (or standing) position, grip the bar with the palms facing downward, wrapping the fingers and thumbs around it. (A) Raise the bar to the shoulders. Extend the wrists, allowing the bar to rest back in the fingers. (B) Keeping the forearms and elbows locked into place, rotate the wrists forward. Return to the starting position.

Scan for Visual

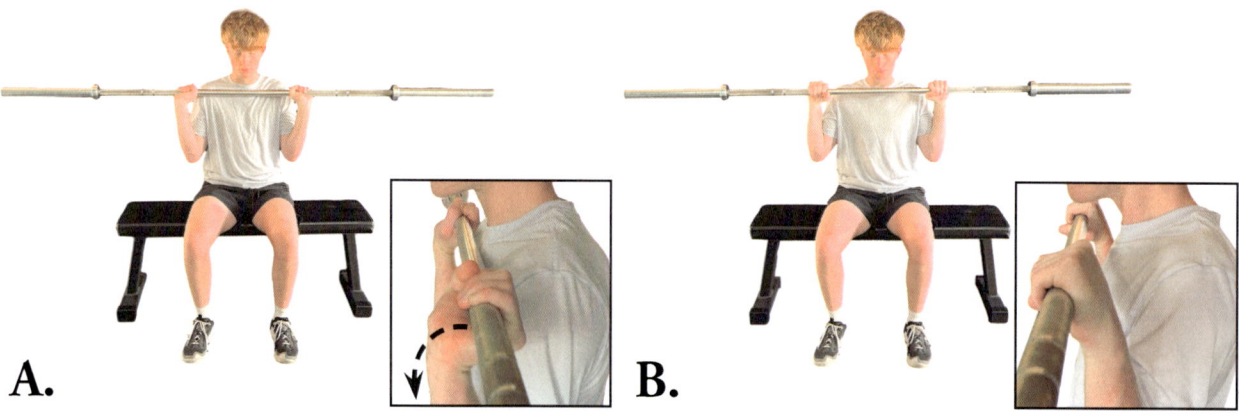

A. B.

STRENGTH TRAINING | 8

ACCESSORY EXERCISES: TRICEPS EXTENSION

EXPLAINED: (A) Using the "Ancore Pro" (from AncoreTraining.com) or an equivalent cable device secured in place overhead, bend the elbows, and grip the triceps rope attachment with both hands. (B) Keeping the elbows locked into place at the side of the ribs, pull the attachment down until full extension of the elbows is achieved. Return to the starting position.

Scan for Visual

A.

B.

ACCESSORY EXERCISES: OVERHEAD TRICEPS EXTENSION

EXPLAINED: (A) Using the "Ancore Pro" (from AncoreTraining.com) or an equivalent cable device secured in place overhead, face away from the cable device. Bend the elbows, and grip the triceps rope attachment with both hands behind the head. (B) With the back slightly bent forward and fixed in place, pull the attachment from behind and over the top of the head until the elbows are fully extended. Return to the starting position.

Scan for Visual

A.

B.

97

DEVELOPING A PITCHER

Programming Resistance Training Workouts and Other Tips

The Lifts are each performed across **3 work-sets** (i.e., *maximum* intensity sets of the *same weight*), with each work-set targeting **5 repetitions**. (This does not count warm-up sets, which <u>absolutely</u> must be done.) When all 5 repetitions of each work-set are successfully done with good form in one session, the work-set weight can be increased at the next session. Bench Press and Press are NEVER done on the same day, so a sample schedule has the following flow over 2 weeks:

Week 1		
Monday	Wednesday	Friday
Squat*	Squat*	Squat*
Bench Press†	Press†	Bench Press†
▪ 3 to 4 warm-up sets for each lift, followed by 3 work-sets of 5 repetitions each		

Week 2		
Monday	Wednesday	Friday
Squat*	Squat*	Squat*
Press†	Bench Press†	Press†
▪ 3 to 4 warm-up sets for each lift, followed by 3 work-sets of 5 repetitions each		

*Myofascial Release and an abbreviated Dynamic Warm-up & Static Stretching routine are performed prior to Squat.

†Arm Bands are performed prior to Bench Press (or Press).

The *Accessory Exercises* are also performed across **three work-sets**, but each work-set here targets **12 to 15 repetitions**. They are integrated during or immediately following the upper body lift of the day and are performed with higher repetitions of lighter weight, so no warm-up sets are required for the *Accessory Exercises*.

The *Accessory Exercises* are typically grouped into pairs, and the 2 paired exercises are performed back-to-back. Wrist Curl and Reverse Wrist Curl are paired together and completed back-to-back between the warm-up sets of the upper body lift. Triceps Extension and Overhead Triceps Extension are paired together and completed back-to-back after *all* other work-sets of the upper body are finished. An example of the flow for a typical strength training day is outlined below:

Sample Workout Day	
Order	Activity
1	Myofascial Release (See Ch. 6)
2	Abbreviated Dynamic Warm-up & Static Stretching Routine (see Ch. 6)
3	Squat ▪ 3 to 4 warm-up sets ▪ 3 work-sets of 5 reps each
4	Arm Bands (see Ch. 6)
5	Bench Press (or Press) ▪ 1st warm-up set
6	Wrist Curl (15 reps) Reverse Wrist Curl (15 reps) (Above sets performed back-to-back)
7	Bench Press (or Press) ▪ 2nd warm-up set
8	Wrist Curl (15 reps) Reverse Wrist Curl (15 reps) (Above sets performed back-to-back)
9	Bench Press (or Press) ▪ 3rd warm-up set
10	Wrist Curl (15 reps) Reverse Wrist Curl (15 reps) (Above sets performed back-to-back)
11	Bench Press (or Press) ▪ 3 work-sets of 5 reps each
12	Triceps Extension (12 reps) Overhead Triceps Extension (12 reps) ▪ Above sets performed as single set back-to-back, for 3 total work-sets (Rest briefly between work-sets)

Programming the above lifts and exercises into a routine that athletes can consistently perform year-round is always challenging. There are many things that compete for their time and attention athletically, academically, and socially, so here are 3 caveats to keep in mind:

- We don't necessarily *schedule* any off-weeks for strength training workouts throughout the year. Life has its own way of throwing you plenty of *off-days*. For a student athlete, this can easily be understood in the case of injury, scheduled vacation, in-season games, or a critical homework assignment that must be finished by a deadline. Days before games are also historically avoided for weightlifting. When significant muscle soreness limits normal movement patterns and flexibility, even after an appropriate warm-up, the athlete needs more recovery time and should wait 48 hours before returning to that scheduled workout. **Days like these become our off-days.**

- The 3 lifts and 4 accessory exercises outlined above are not the ONLY weightlifting activities that can be helpful for developing generalized strength in a pitcher from youth to high school. As an example, our highly coveted summer off-season training programs incorporate deadlifts, power cleans, and other ancillary speed and power building routines. However, it is exceedingly rare that players at our level have the time to perform all these exercises year-round. If they do, they are most likely training to be a powerlifter, and not a pitcher, as the latter also needs time to complete highly important sport-specific activities like the *Arm Care & Velo Program* and *Bullpen Pitching*. Ultimately, when it comes to strength training at the levels we are discussing, it is far better to learn how to do a few lifts really well than numerous lifts marginally. The program previously outlined in this chapter will help the majority of pitchers meet their strength goals if they perform it consistently throughout the year.

- You do not have to complete all the scheduled lifts and accessory exercises EVERY weightlifting day. Yes, if you skip more sets than you perform, you will fail to progress, but there will be some portions of the year when time constraints on a given strength training day are just insurmountable. Do not let this stop you from doing *something*. On these days, reduce the number of work-sets for a given lift from 3 to 2, or perform the squat and bench press only, and then be done for the day. Modifying the duration of things from time to time is acceptable and sometimes needed to maintain consistency. This approach will drive the needle further than lengthy workouts done infrequently.

In the chapter that follows, you will find detailed workout templates—along with specific player examples—to best illustrate how to integrate all the programs in this book at the various seasons of the year.

9
Workout Templates

> "
> We are what we repeatedly do. Excellence
> then, is not an act, but a habit.
> —Aristotle

The following templates are provided as a guide for programming workouts throughout the year for youth to high school players. They outline a general approach for integrating pitching-specific training (e.g., the *Arm Care & Velo Program*) with generalized performance training (e.g., the *Strength Program*). The templates are organized into **Off-Season**, **Pre-Season**, and **In-Season**, starting with the workouts most applicable for the middle school and high school-age levels. Actual workouts completed by real players, including their weights and repetitions, are also included to better convey real-life workflows. As previously discussed, the number of repetitions recommended for each exercise and activity is meant only as a guide, and may need to be modified for an individual player from time to time.

DEVELOPING A PITCHER

OFF-SEASON TEMPLATE

OFF-SEASON PROGRAM OVERVIEW

The off-season is primarily geared toward building up generalized strength and arm velocity, so this portion of the year has the highest percentage of total training time (approximately 50%, or 3 days per week) devoted to the *Strength Program*. It is recommended that pitchers also devote 3 days per week to the pitching-specific *Arm Care & Velo Program*, which will include a mixture of *Standard*, *Flat-Ground Pitching*, and *Bullpen Pitching* days. A sample overview of the off-season is outlined here:

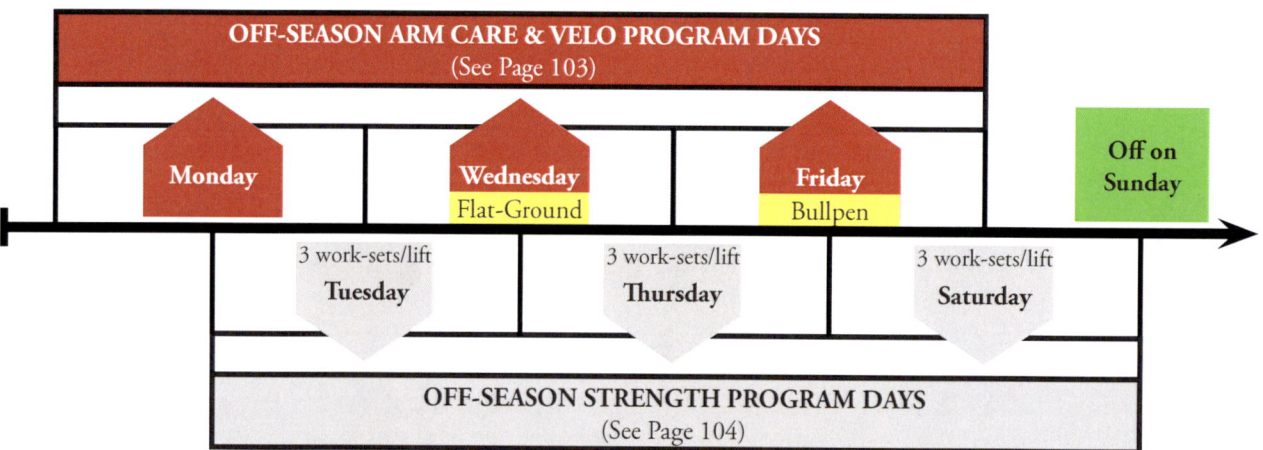

BULLPEN PITCHING NOTES Given its focus on strength training, the off-season *Arm Care & Velo Program* generally has the least percentage of total time devoted to *Bullpen Pitching* (at ≤ 1 day/week). The sample template provided on the adjacent page (p. 103) includes an off-season week consisting of one *Standard*, one *Flat-Ground Pitching*, and one *Bullpen Pitching* day. In some off-season weeks, our pitchers will only perform *Standard* and/or *Flat-Ground Pitching* days, with the latter being done the most when pitchers are learning new pitch-types and grips.

STRENGTH PROGRAM NOTES When 3 work-sets of 5 repetitions for any of *The Lifts* can be performed successfully (with good form) in a single session, weight can be increased in that lift for the next session. The *Accessory Exercises* are performed with higher numbers of repetitions (12 to 15), but the same premise applies: weight can be added to an exercise when *all* repetitions can be done for every work-set.

The off-season workouts of an actual pitcher are shown on page 105. They include one *Arm Care & Velo Program* day with *Flat-Ground Pitching*, and one *Strength Program* day with Squat and Bench Press.

WORKOUT TEMPLATES | 9

MIDDLE / HIGH SCHOOL

OFF-SEASON ARM CARE & VELO PROGRAM WEEK

	Standard Day†	Flat-Ground Pitching Day†	Bullpen Pitching Day†
	Monday	**Wednesday**	**Friday**
Myofascial Release	Back, Glutes, Hamstrings, Calves, Quadriceps, Groin/Adductors, Latissimus Dorsi, Deltoids, Lateral Chest		
Arm Bands	Elevated Internal & External Rotation, Forward Flies, Reverse Flies, Internal Rotation at Hip, External Rotation at Hip, Standing "Y", Back Rows, Statue of Liberty		
Dynamic Warm-up/Stretch	High Knees, Bottom Kickers, Knee Huggers, Cradle Walks, Lunges with Twist, Side Lunges, Groin Stretches		
Plyo Balls and Throws	**Reverse Throws**: Green Ball (32 oz) x 10, Blue Ball (21 oz) x 10		
	Twist & Throws: Blue Ball (21 oz) x 10, Yellow Ball (14 oz) x 10		
	Hip Finishers: Red Ball (7 oz) x 15 or **Hip Finishers with Core Velocity Belt**: Red Ball (7 oz) Black Tension Band x 5, Blue Tension Band x 5, No Tension Band x 5		
	Weigh Mores: Purple Ball (5 oz) x 20 or **Weigh Mores with Core Velocity Belt**: Purple Ball (5 oz) Black Tension Band x 5 No Tension Band x 5 Blue Tension Band x 5 No Tension Band x 5	**Weigh Mores**: Purple Ball (5 oz) x 15 or **Weigh Mores with Core Velocity Belt**: Purple Ball (5 oz) Black Tension Band x 5 Blue Tension Band x 5 No Tension Band x 5	**Whip Behinds**: Standard Baseball x 5 **Cloud Touches**: Standard Baseball x 5
	Whip Behinds: Standard Baseball x 10 **Cloud Touches**: Standard Baseball x 10	**Whip Behinds**: Standard Baseball x 5 **Cloud Touches**: Standard Baseball x 5	**Bullpen Pitching***: Fastballs x 10 Changeups x 10 Curveballs x 10 Sliders x 10 Group of 4 (Fastball, Changeup, Curveball, Slider) x 2 sets
		Flat-Ground Pitching*: Fastballs x 10 Changeups x 10 Curveballs x 10 Sliders x 10	
Cooldown: Wrist Weights	**Presses**: Wrist Weight (5 lb) Each Wrist x 60 sec **Bent-Over Rows**: Wrist Weight (5 lb) Each Wrist x 50 reps **Rotational Presses**: Wrist Weight (5 lb) Each Wrist x 25 reps **Elevated Arm Hold**: Wrist Weight (10 lb) on Throwing Wrist x 60 sec		
Cooldown: Heavy Ball	**Horizontal Ball Hold**: Black Ball (4.4 lb or 2000 g) x 60 sec **Kneeling Ball Hold**: Black Ball (4.4 lb or 2000 g) x 60 sec		

*Modify if there are less, more, or other pitch-types being practiced.

ARM CARE & VELO PROGRAM

†All 3 days of some weeks can be *Standard* or *Flat-Ground Pitching*, or all 3 days can be alternated between those two.

103

DEVELOPING A PITCHER

OFF-SEASON TEMPLATE (CONT.)

OFF-SEASON STRENGTH PROGRAM WEEK

	Squat & Bench Press* + Accessory Exercises		Squat & Press* + Accessory Exercises		Squat & Bench Press* + Accessory Exercises		
	Tuesday		**Thursday**		**Saturday**		
Myofascial Release	Back, Glutes, Hamstrings, Calves, Quadriceps, Groin/Adductors, Latissimus Dorsi, Deltoids, Lateral Chest						
Dynamic Warm-up/Stretch	High Knees, Bottom Kickers, Knee Huggers, Cradle Walks, Lunges with Twist, Side Lunges, Groin Stretches						S T R E N G T H P R O G R A M
Lower Body	**Squat** Warm-up: 3-4 sets		**Squat** Warm-up: 3-4 sets		**Squat** Warm-up: 3-4 sets		
	Squat Work-sets: 3 sets x 5 reps		**Squat** Work-sets: 3 sets x 5 reps		**Squat** Work-sets: 3 sets x 5 reps		
Arm Bands	Elevated Internal Rotation, Elevated External Rotation, Forward Flies, Reverse Flies, Internal Rotation at Hip, External Rotation at Hip, Standing "Y", Back Rows						
Upper Body	**Bench Press*** Warm-up: 3-4 Sets	**Wrist Curl**†: 3 sets x 15 reps **Reverse Wrist Curl**†: 3 sets x 15 reps	**Press*** Warm-up: 3-4 Sets	**Wrist Curl**†: 3 sets x 15 reps **Reverse Wrist Curl**†: 3 sets x 15 reps	**Bench Press*** Warm-up: 3-4 Sets	**Wrist Curl**†: 3 sets x 15 reps **Reverse Wrist Curl**†: 3 sets x 15 reps	
	Bench Press* Work-sets: 3 sets x 5 reps		**Press*** Work-sets: 3 sets x 5 reps		**Bench Press*** Work-sets: 3 sets x 5 reps		
	Triceps Extension (TE) & Overhead TE 3 sets x 12 reps of each		**Triceps Extension (TE) & Overhead TE** 3 sets x 12 reps of each		**Triceps Extension (TE) & Overhead TE** 3 sets x 12 reps of each		

*Alternate days with Bench Press and Press. For example, Week 1 is shown above with Bench Press on Tuesday, Press on Thursday, and Bench Press on Saturday. Week 2 would be Press on Tuesday, Bench Press on Thursday, and Press on Saturday.

†Perform the paired set of Wrist Curl and Reverse Wrist Curl back-to-back in between upper body warm-up sets.

WORKOUT TEMPLATES | 9

MIDDLE / HIGH SCHOOL

SAMPLE ATHLETE WORKOUTS

5'9" 148 lbs Male

Off-Season Arm Care & Velo Program: Flat-Ground Pitching Day
(Numbers without units represent throws performed)

Myofascial Release	Arm Bands	Dynamic Warm-Up	Plyo Ball Throws	Whip Behinds	Cloud Touches	Flat-Ground Pitching	Cooldown

✓	✓	✓	**Reverse Throws:**
			-Green (32 oz) x 10
			-Blue (21 oz) x 10
			Twist & Throws:
			-Blue (21 oz) x 10
			-Yellow (14 oz) x 10
			Hip Finishers w/ Core Velocity Belt (CVB):
			-Red Ball (7 oz):
			  Black Tension Band x 5
			  Blue Tension Band x 5
			  No Tension Band x 5
			Weigh Mores w/ CVB:
			-Purple Ball (5 oz):
			  Black Tension Band x 5
			  Blue Tension Band x 5
			  No Tension Band x 5
				5	5	-**Fastballs** x 10
						
						-**Changeups** x 10
						
						-**Curveballs** x 10
						
						-**Sliders** x 10
							-**Presses**: 60 secs
							-**Bent-Over Rows**: 50 reps
							-**Rotational Presses**: 25 reps
							-**Elevated Arm Hold**: 60 secs
							-**Horizontal Ball Hold**: 60 secs
							-**Kneeling Ball Hold**: 60 secs
							-**Light Jog**: 2 miles

Off-Season Strength Program: Squat & Bench Press Day
(Format: Weight x Repetitions x Sets)

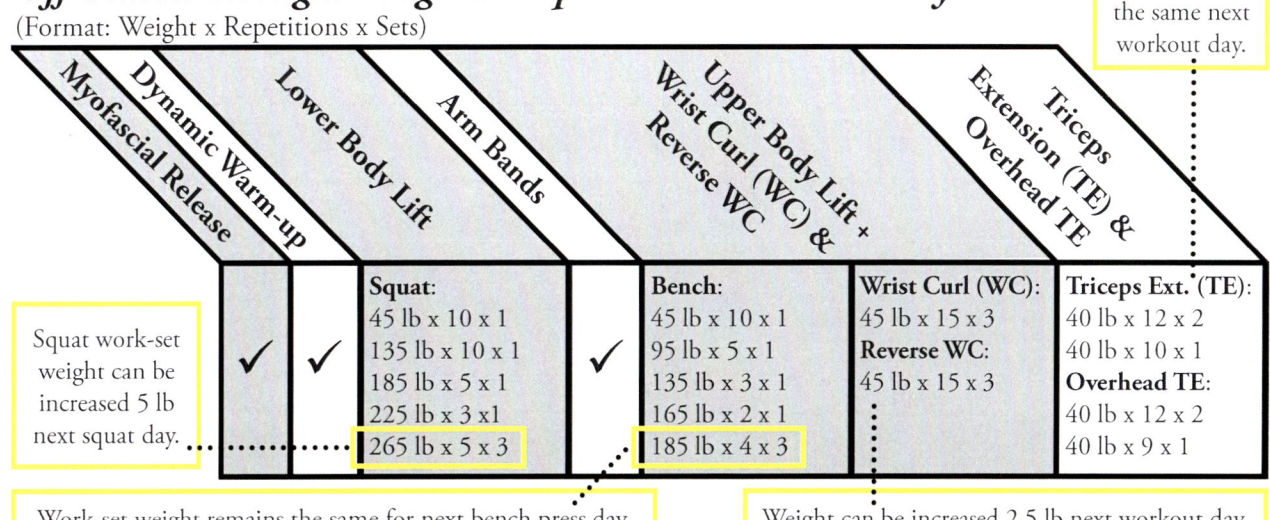

Myofascial Release	Dynamic Warm-up	Lower Body Lift	Arm Bands	Upper Body Lift + Wrist Curl (WC) & Reverse WC	Triceps Extension (TE) & Overhead TE
✓	✓	**Squat:** 45 lb x 10 x 1 135 lb x 10 x 1 185 lb x 5 x 1 225 lb x 3 x 1 **265 lb x 5 x 3**	✓	**Bench:** 45 lb x 10 x 1 95 lb x 5 x 1 135 lb x 3 x 1 165 lb x 2 x 1 **185 lb x 4 x 3** **Wrist Curl (WC):** 45 lb x 15 x 3 **Reverse WC:** 45 lb x 15 x 3	**Triceps Ext. (TE):** 40 lb x 12 x 2 40 lb x 10 x 1 **Overhead TE:** 40 lb x 12 x 2 40 lb x 9 x 1

Squat work-set weight can be increased 5 lb next squat day.

Work-set weight remains the same for next bench press day.

Weight can be increased 2.5 lb next workout day.

Weight remains the same next workout day.

DEVELOPING A PITCHER

PRE-SEASON TEMPLATE

PRE-SEASON PROGRAM OVERVIEW

We designate the pre-season as the 4 weeks leading up to the start of in-season team practices. The *Strength Program* in the pre-season continues at 3 days per week, but the number of work-sets performed for each of *The Lifts* is reduced from 3 to 2. This helps to balance the rising intensity of the *Arm Care & Velo Program* at this time of the year due to more frequent *Bullpen Pitching* (2 days per week). A sample overview of the pre-season is outlined here:

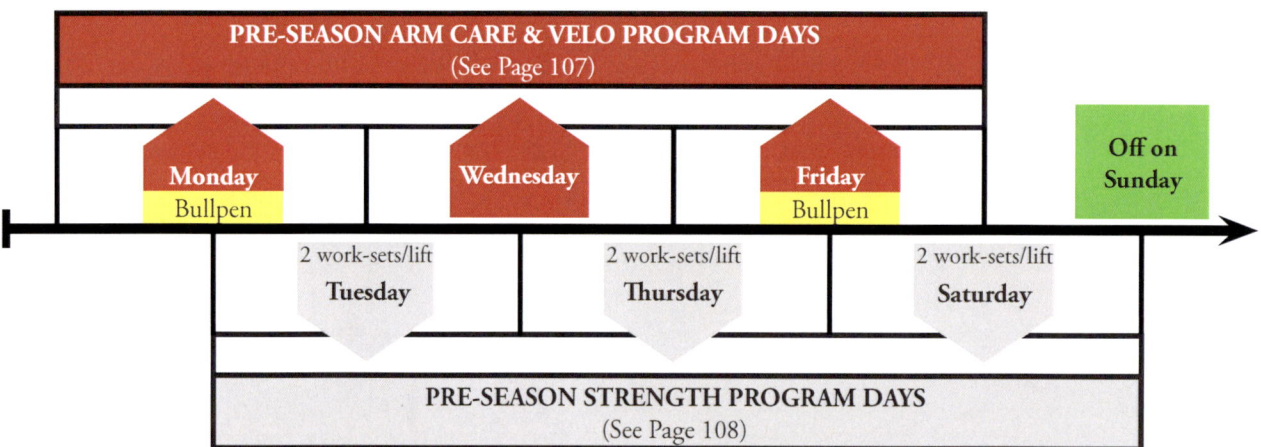

BULLPEN PITCHING NOTES The transition from the off-season to the pre-season is marked by an increase in *Bullpen Pitching* days to twice weekly. The sample template provided on the adjacent page (p. 107) includes a pre-season week with 2 *Bullpen Pitching* days, one being lighter in pitch count than the other. The total pitch count for bullpen sessions is ramped up each week over the course of the pre-season.

STRENGTH PROGRAM NOTES When 2 work-sets of 5 repetitions for one of *The Lifts* can be performed successfully (with good form) in a single session, weight can be increased in that lift for the next session. The *Accessory Exercises* are performed with higher numbers of repetitions (12 to 15), but the same premise applies: weight can be added in an exercise when *all* repetitions can be done for every work-set.

The pre-season workouts of an actual pitcher are shown on page 109. They include one *Arm Care & Velo Program* day with *Bullpen Pitching*, and one *Strength Program* day with Squat and Bench Press.

WORKOUT TEMPLATES | 9

MIDDLE / HIGH SCHOOL

PRE-SEASON ARM CARE & VELO PROGRAM WEEK

	Bullpen Pitching Day **Monday**	Standard Day **Wednesday**	Bullpen Pitching Day **Friday**
Myofascial Release	Back, Glutes, Hamstrings, Calves, Quadriceps, Groin/Adductors, Latissimus Dorsi, Deltoids, Lateral Chest		
Arm Bands	Elevated Internal & External Rotation, Forward Flies, Reverse Flies, Internal Rotation at Hip, External Rotation at Hip, Standing "Y", Back Rows, Statue of Liberty		
Dynamic Warm-up/Stretch	High Knees, Bottom Kickers, Knee Huggers, Cradle Walks, Lunges with Twist, Side Lunges, Groin Stretches		
Plyo Balls and Throws	**Reverse Throws**: Green Ball (32 oz) x 10, Blue Ball (21 oz) x 10 **Twist & Throws**: Blue Ball (21 oz) x 10, Yellow Ball (14 oz) x 10 **Hip Finishers**: Red Ball (7 oz) x 15 or **Hip Finishers with Core Velocity Belt**: Red Ball (7 oz) Black Tension Band x 5, Blue Tension Band x 5, No Tension Band x 5		
	Whip Behinds: Standard Baseball x 5 **Cloud Touches**: Standard Baseball x 5 **Bullpen Pitching***: Fastballs x 10 Changeups x 10 Curveballs x 10 Group of 3 (Fastball, Changeup, Curveball) x 3 sets	**Weigh Mores**: Purple Ball (5 oz) x 15 or **Weigh Mores with Core Velocity Belt**: Purple Ball (5 oz) Black Tension Band x 5 Blue Tension Band x 5 No Tension Band x 5 **Whip Behinds**: Standard Baseball x 10 **Cloud Touches**: Standard Baseball x 10	**Whip Behinds**: Standard Baseball x 5 **Cloud Touches**: Standard Baseball x 5 **Bullpen Pitching***: Fastballs x 10 Changeups x 10 Curveballs x 10 Group of 3 (Fastball, Changeup, Curveball) x 5 sets
Cooldown: Wrist Weights	**Presses**: Wrist Weight (5 lb) Each Wrist x 60 sec **Bent-Over Rows**: Wrist Weight (5 lb) Each Wrist x 50 reps **Rotational Presses**: Wrist Weight (5 lb) Each Wrist x 25 reps **Elevated Arm Hold**: Wrist Weight (10 lb) on Throwing Wrist x 60 sec		
Cooldown: Heavy Ball	**Horizontal Ball Hold**: Black Ball (4.4 lb or 2000 g) x 60 sec **Kneeling Ball Hold**: Black Ball (4.4 lb or 2000 g) x 60 sec		

*Modify if there are less, more, or other pitch-types being practiced.

ARM CARE & VELO PROGRAM

DEVELOPING A PITCHER

PRE-SEASON TEMPLATE (CONT.)

PRE-SEASON STRENGTH PROGRAM WEEK

	Squat & Bench Press* + Accessory Exercises	Squat & Press* + Accessory Exercises	Squat & Bench Press* + Accessory Exercises	
	Tuesday	**Thursday**	**Saturday**	
Myofascial Release	Back, Glutes, Hamstrings, Calves, Quadriceps, Groin/Adductors, Latissimus Dorsi, Deltoids, Lateral Chest			
Dynamic Warm-up/Stretch	High Knees, Bottom Kickers, Knee Huggers, Cradle Walks, Lunges with Twist, Side Lunges, Groin Stretches			
Lower Body	**Squat** Warm-up: 3-4 sets	**Squat** Warm-up: 3-4 sets	**Squat** Warm-up: 3-4 sets	**STRENGTH PROGRAM**
	Squat Work-sets: 2 sets x 5 reps	**Squat** Work-sets: 2 sets x 5 reps	**Squat** Work-sets: 2 sets x 5 reps	
Arm Bands	Elevated Internal Rotation, Elevated External Rotation, Forward Flies, Reverse Flies, Internal Rotation at Hip, External Rotation at Hip, Standing "Y", Back Rows			
Upper Body	**Bench Press*** Warm-up: 3-4 Sets / **Wrist Curl†**: 3 sets x 15 reps **Reverse Wrist Curl†**: 3 sets x 15 reps	**Press*** Warm-up: 3-4 Sets / **Wrist Curl†**: 3 sets x 15 reps **Reverse Wrist Curl†**: 3 sets x 15 reps	**Bench Press*** Warm-up: 3-4 Sets / **Wrist Curl†**: 3 sets x 15 reps **Reverse Wrist Curl†**: 3 sets x 15 reps	
	Bench Press* Work-sets: 2 sets x 5 reps	**Press*** Work-sets: 2 sets x 5 reps	**Bench Press*** Work-sets: 2 sets x 5 reps	
	Triceps Extension (TE) & Overhead TE 3 sets x 12 reps of each	**Triceps Extension (TE) & Overhead TE** 3 sets x 12 reps of each	**Triceps Extension (TE) & Overhead TE** 3 sets x 12 reps of each	

*Alternate days with Bench Press and Press. For example, Week 1 is shown above with Bench Press on Tuesday, Press on Thursday, and Bench Press on Saturday. Week 2 would be Press on Tuesday, Bench Press on Thursday, and Press on Saturday.

†Perform the paired set of Wrist Curl and Reverse Wrist Curl back-to-back in between upper body warm-up sets.

WORKOUT TEMPLATES | 9

MIDDLE / HIGH SCHOOL

SAMPLE ATHLETE WORKOUTS

5'9" 148 lbs Male

Pre-Season Arm Care & Velo Program: Bullpen Pitching Day
(Numbers without units represent throws performed)

Myofascial Release	Arm Bands	Dynamic Warm-Up	Plyo Ball Throws	Whip Behinds	Cloud Touches	Bullpen Pitching	Cooldown

✓	✓	✓	**Reverse Throws:**
			-Green (32 oz) x 10
			-Blue (21 oz) x 10
			
			Twist & Throws:
			-Blue (21 oz) x 10
			-Yellow (14 oz) x 10
			
			Hip Finishers w/ Core Velocity Belt (CVB):
			-Red Ball (7 oz):
			  Black Tension Band x 5
			  Blue Tension Band x 5
			  No Tension Band x 5
				5	5	**-Fastballs** x 10
						
						-Changeups x 10
						
						-Curveballs x 10
						
						-Group of 3
						(Fastball, Changeup, Curveball) x 5 Sets
							-**Presses**: 60 secs
							
							-**Bent-Over Rows**: 50 reps
							
							-**Rotational Presses**: 25 reps
							
							-**Elevated Arm Hold**: 60 secs
							
							-**Horizontal Ball Hold**: 60 secs
							
							-**Kneeling Ball Hold**: 60 secs

Pre-Season Strength Program: Squat & Bench Press Day
(Format: Weight x Repetitions x Sets)

Myofascial Release	Dynamic Warm-up	Lower Body Lift	Arm Bands	Upper Body Lift + Wrist Curl (WC) & Reverse WC	Triceps Extension (TE) & Overhead TE
✓	✓	**Squat:** 45 lb x 10 x 1 135 lb x 10 x 1 185 lb x 5 x 1 225 lb x 3 x 1 **255 lb x 5 x 2**	✓	**Bench:** 45 lb x 10 x 1 95 lb x 5 x 1 135 lb x 3 x 1 160 lb x 2 x 1 **180 lb x 4 x 2** **Wrist Curl (WC):** 42 lb x 15 x 3 **Reverse WC:** 42 lb x 15 x 3	**Triceps Ext. (TE):** 35 lb x 12 x 3 **Overhead TE:** 35 lb x 12 x 3

Weight can be increased next workout day.

Squat work-set weight can be increased 5 lb next squat day.

Work-set weight remains the same for next bench press day.

Weight can be increased 2.5 lb next workout day.

DEVELOPING A PITCHER

IN-SEASON TEMPLATE

IN-SEASON PROGRAM OVERVIEW

During the in-season, the plan is simple: *Strength Program* (2 days per week), warm-up/cooldown routines of the *Arm Care & Velo Program* (5-6 days per week), and *Bullpen Pitching* (2 days per week). A sample overview of a spring high school baseball season with 2 weekday games is outlined here:

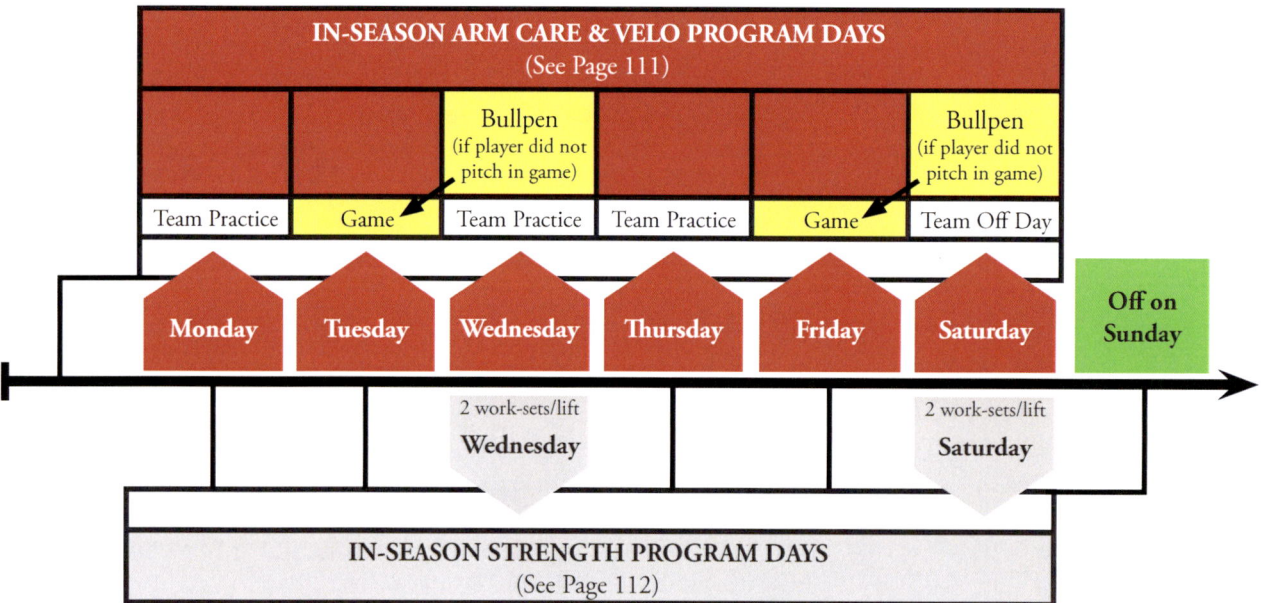

When in-season games fall on a Friday through Sunday in a given week (e.g., tournament weekend or summer season), the *Strength Program* days typically shift to Mondays and Wednesdays, and the mid-week bullpen day to Tuesdays.

BULLPEN PITCHING NOTES Throughout the in-season, *Bullpen Pitching* is performed 2 days per week. Pitching in a game is almost always equivalent to a bullpen and should be counted as one. The sample template provided on the adjacent page (p. 111) includes an in-season week with 2 days of *Bullpen Pitching*. They should be performed only when a player did not pitch in a game on the day before.

STRENGTH PROGRAM NOTES The in-season *Strength Program* primarily focuses on "maintenance." While some players may still gain strength if training time allows, most pitchers should fix their work-set weight (i.e., avoid increasing weight) and perform one upper-body and one lower-body lift twice per week.

The in-season workouts of an actual pitcher are shown on page 113. They include one *Arm Care & Velo Program* day with *Bullpen Pitching*, and one *Strength Program* day with Squat and Bench Press.

MIDDLE / HIGH SCHOOL

IN-SEASON ARM CARE & VELO PROGRAM WEEK

	Monday†	Tuesday†	Wednesday†	Thursday†	Friday†	Saturday†
Arm Bands	Elevated Internal & External Rotation, Forward Flies, Reverse Flies, Internal Rotation at Hip, External Rotation at Hip, Standing "Y", Back Rows, Statue of Liberty					
Team Warm-up	Should include the equivalent of a Dynamic Warm-up & Stretching Routine					
Team Activities	Practice	Game	Practice	Practice	Game	Team Off Day
Bullpen‡ ‡Only perform when a player did not pitch in a game on the day before. *Modify if there are less, more, or other pitch-types being practiced.	X	X	**Bullpen Pitching***: Fastballs x 5 Changeups x 5 Curveballs x 5 Group of 3 (Fastball, Changeup, Curveball) x 5 sets	X	X	**Bullpen Pitching***: Fastballs x 10 Changeups x 10 Curveballs x 10 Group of 3 (Fastball, Changeup, Curveball) x 5 sets
Cooldown: Wrist Weights	**Presses**: Wrist Weight (5 lb) Each Wrist x 60 sec **Bent-Over Rows**: Wrist Weight (5 lb) Each Wrist x 50 reps **Rotational Presses**: Wrist Weight (5 lb) Each Wrist x 25 reps **Elevated Arm Hold**: Wrist Weight (10 lb) on Throwing Wrist x 60 sec					
Cooldown: Heavy Ball	**Horizontal Ball Hold**: Black Ball (4.4 lb or 2000 g) x 60 sec **Kneeling Ball Hold**: Black Ball (4.4 lb or 2000 g) x 60 sec					
	X = OFF					

†If in-season games fall on a Friday through Sunday in a given week (e.g., tournament weekend or summer season), the mid-week *Bullpen Pitching* day on Wednesday would typically shift to Tuesday.

Note: Pitching in a game is almost always equivalent to a bullpen and should be counted as one.

DEVELOPING A PITCHER

IN-SEASON TEMPLATE (CONT.)

IN-SEASON STRENGTH PROGRAM WEEK

	Squat & Bench Press* + Accessory Exercises††	Squat & Bench Press* + Accessory Exercises††	
	Wednesday†	**Saturday†**	
Myofascial Release	Back, Glutes, Hamstrings, Calves, Quadriceps, Groin/Adductors, Latissimus Dorsi, Deltoids, Lateral Chest		**STRENGTH PROGRAM**
Dynamic Warm-up/Stretch	High Knees, Bottom Kickers, Knee Huggers, Cradle Walks, Lunges with Twist, Side Lunges, Groin Stretches		
Lower Body	**Squat** Warm-up: 3-4 sets	**Squat** Warm-up: 3-4 sets	
	Squat Work-sets: 2 sets x 5 reps	**Squat** Work-sets: 2 sets x 5 reps	
Arm Bands	Elevated Internal Rotation, Elevated External Rotation, Forward Flies, Reverse Flies, Internal Rotation at Hip, External Rotation at Hip, Standing Y, Back Rows		
Upper Body	**Bench Press*** Warm-up: 3-4 Sets	**Wrist Curl‡:** 3 sets x 15 reps **Reverse Wrist Curl‡:** 3 sets x 15 reps	**Bench Press*** Warm-up: 3-4 Sets	**Wrist Curl‡:** 3 sets x 15 reps **Reverse Wrist Curl‡:** 3 sets x 15 reps	
	Bench Press* Work-sets: 2 sets x 5 reps	**Bench Press*** Work-sets: 2 sets x 5 reps	
	Triceps Extension (TE) & Overhead TE 3 sets x 12 reps of each	**Triceps Extension (TE) & Overhead TE** 3 sets x 12 reps of each	

*For most pitchers during the in-season, the best approach is to fix their work-set weight (i.e., not attempt to increase it) and only perform one upper-body lift (bench press) and one lower-body lift (squat) up to twice weekly. Maintaining most of the strength built in the prior off-season and pre-season will help players to start ahead and make greater gains in the upcoming off-season.

†If in-season games are scheduled on a Friday through Sunday in a given week (e.g., tournament weekend or summer season), the *Strength Program* days would typically shift to Mondays and Wednesdays.

‡Perform the paired set of Wrist Curl and Reverse Wrist Curl back-to-back in between upper body warm-up sets.

WORKOUT TEMPLATES | 9

MIDDLE / HIGH SCHOOL

SAMPLE ATHLETE WORKOUTS

5'9" 148 lbs Male

In-Season Arm Care & Velo Program: Mid-Week Bullpen Pitching Day
(Numbers without units represent throws performed)

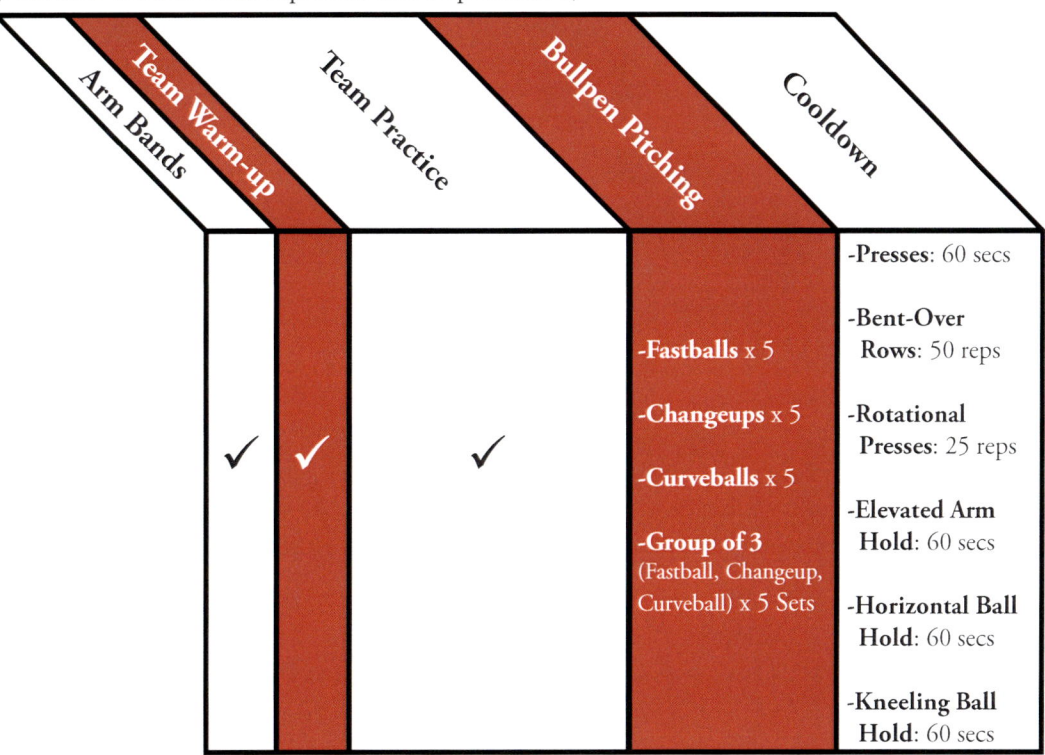

In-Season Strength Program: Saturday Squat & Bench Press Day
(Format: Weight x Repetitions x Sets)

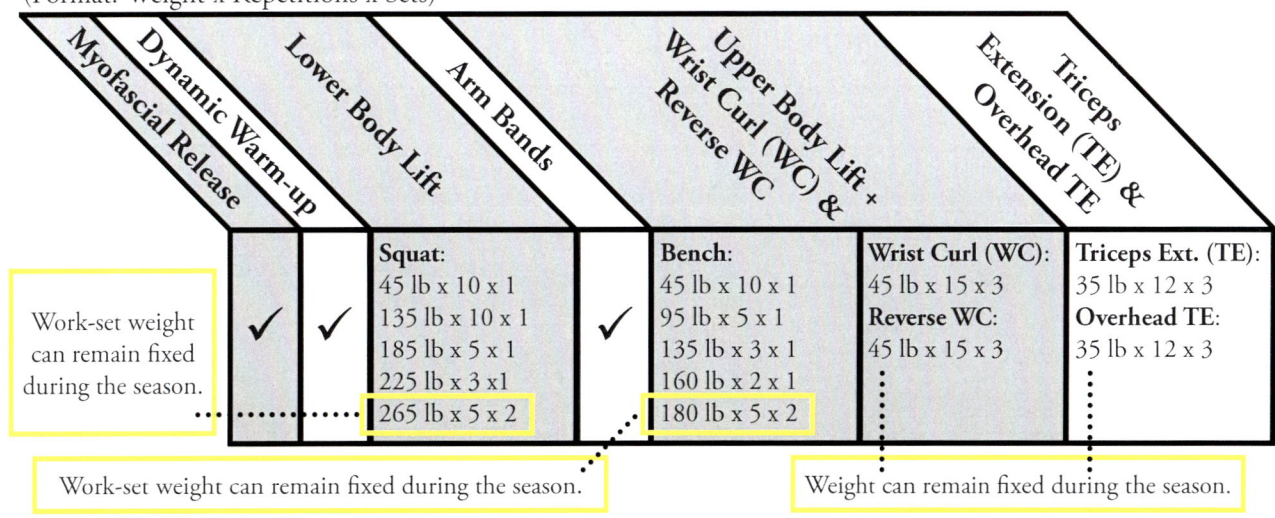

113

DEVELOPING A PITCHER

TEMPLATES FOR YOUNGER YOUTH

COMMENTS ABOUT AN OFF-SEASON PROGRAM FOR YOUNGER YOUTH

As discussed in Chapter 4, younger pitchers (elementary school-age) should naturally have breaks in their baseball training schedules throughout the year. At this level, we strongly encourage other non-baseball sports participation in the off-season. This does not mean that younger players cannot throw a baseball during this time. We would just prefer that players at this age spend their time practicing other sports for broader athletic development, at least until it makes sense for them (if they so choose) to specialize in baseball at a later date.

For this very reason, we don't specifically provide an off-season baseball template that incorporates an *Arm Care & Velo Program* for younger youth to follow. Instead, we only recommend that they perform a *Strength Program* (Chapter 8) using bodyweight exercises in the off-season or year-round.

IN-SEASON PROGRAM OVERVIEW FOR YOUNGER YOUTH

The in-season program for younger pitchers (elementary school-age) includes up to 3 days per week of baseball-specific activities (e.g., team practices, individual lessons, or bullpen work) and up to 3 days per week of bodyweight strength training combined with pitching-specific muscle memory drills. A sample in-season overview for younger pitchers is outlined here:

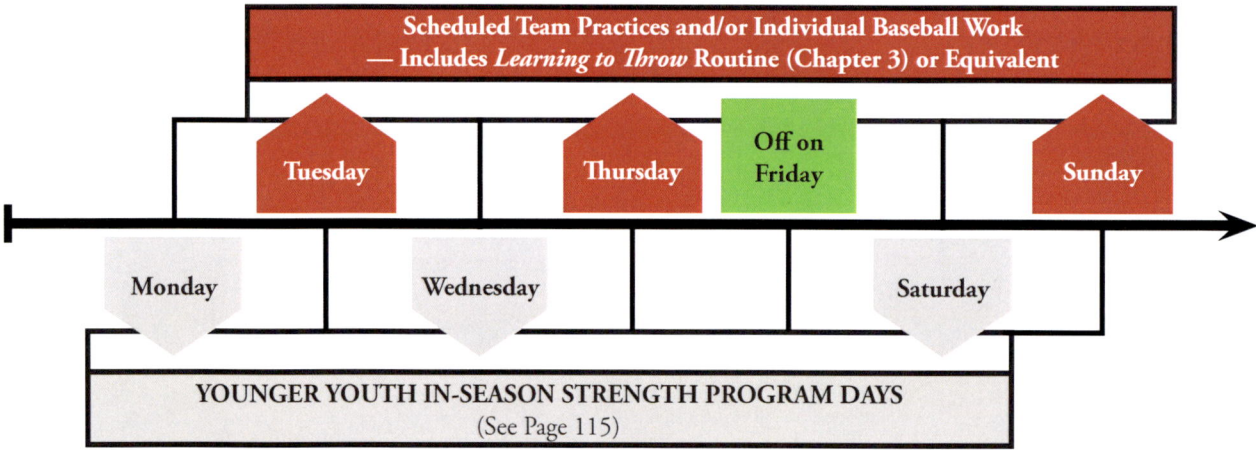

The sample weekly template provided on the adjacent page (p. 115) includes an in-season *Strength Program* for younger pitchers incorporating the *Learning to Pitch* drills.

WORKOUT TEMPLATES | 9

ELEMENTARY SCHOOL

YOUNGER YOUTH IN-SEASON PROGRAM

Bodyweight Strength Program + *Learning to Pitch* Drills

	Monday	Wednesday	Saturday	
Dynamic Warm-up/Stretch		High Knees, Bottom Kickers, Knee Huggers, Cradle Walks, Lunges with Twist, Side Lunges, Groin Stretches, Spiders, Arm Circles & Flaps, Pull Across & Pull Behinds, Shoulder Lifts		

Bodyweight Strength Program

Monday:
- **Ball Pick-Ups:** 40 Reps Total
  - 2 Sets x 10 (Right Leg)
  - 2 Sets x 10 (Left Leg)
- **Bulgarian Split Squats:** 60 Reps Total
  - 3 Sets x 10 (Right Leg)
  - 3 Sets x 10 (Left Leg)
- **Squats:** 36 Reps Total
  - 3 Sets x 12

Wednesday:
- **Single-Leg Glute Bridges:** 60 Reps Total
  - 3 Sets x 10 (Right Leg)
  - 3 Sets x 10 (Left Leg)
- **Push-Ups:** Draw 8 Cards*
- **Sit-Ups:** Draw 8 Cards*

Saturday:
- **Ball Pick-Ups:** 40 Reps Total
  - 2 Sets x 10 (Right Leg)
  - 2 Sets x 10 (Left Leg)
- **Bulgarian Split Squats:** 60 Reps Total
  - 3 Sets x 10 (Right Leg)
  - 3 Sets x 10 (Left Leg)
- **Squats:** 36 Reps Total
  - 3 Sets x 12
- **Single-Leg Glute Bridges:** 60 Reps Total
  - 3 Sets x 10 (Right Leg)
  - 3 Sets x 10 (Left Leg)
- **Push-Ups:** Draw 8 Cards*
- **Sit-Ups:** Draw 8 Cards*

STRENGTH PROGRAM

Learning to Pitch Drills

- **4-Step Windup & Balance Drill:** 10 Reps
- **Separation Drill:** 10 Reps
- **Noes Over Toes Drill:** 10 Reps
- **Tape Down the Mound Drill:** 10 Reps
- **Chest Over Knee Drill:** 10 Reps
- **Glove-Side Tuck Drill:** 10 Reps
- **Towel Extension Drill:** 10 Reps

*Draw a random card from a deck of standard playing cards and perform the exercise for the number of repetitions specified on the card. Aces are 25. Face cards are 10. Numbered cards are their numbers.

Acknowledgments

We wanted to express our sincere gratitude to the following individuals for their important contributions to this book:

To Eva Dorman—for your professional photographs used for the full-page images in Chapter 3 (p. 12), Chapter 4 (p. 20), Chapter 5 (p. 34), Chapter 6 (p. 44), Chapter 7 (p. 68), and Chapter 9 (p. 116).

To Lindsey L. Bilhartz—for your professional photograph used for the full-page image in Chapter 2 (p. 4), for your careful review of this manuscript, and for your myriad seen but largely unrecognized contributions to HUSTLE3.

To Matt Langwell—for MLB Spring Training access and your ongoing professional collaboration in the *early years* when we were developing our training programs.

To "Papa Terry"—for first showing us by example, and then teaching us prior to your passing how to become an author. TDB Field at H3 will forever have your name.

To the numerous athletes, pitchers, players, and teams who have received instruction at HUSTLE3: You have been our inspiration for writing, and if you remain *hungry* for training, we will always have something for you.

About the Authors

Preston B. Bilhartz is a senior in the graduating class of 2026 at Brazos Christian High School in Bryan, Texas, and has been training at HUSTLE3 since 2020. He's participated in Little League and select/travel baseball since age 7, and is currently a high school pitcher at the TAPPS Division III level. A letterman on the varsity baseball team since his freshman year, Preston has pitched more total innings than any other player on his team over his high school career. He was awarded his team's "Most Valuable Pitcher" honor as a sophomore, compiling a 2.85 earned run average (ERA) in 34.1 innings pitched, with 22 strikeouts, 14 walks, and a 63% strike percentage. As a junior, he received his team's "Eagle Teammate Award," given to the player that consistently performs best in pressure situations, finishing with a 1.54 ERA in 31.2 innings pitched, with 27 strikeouts, 16 walks, 0.190 batting average against, and a 64% strike percentage. Preston has also served as an assistant coach for the Brazos Valley Bucks 15U (a select/travel baseball team), and is interested in pursuing a degree in Sports Media and Journalism with his future collegiate studies. When he's not athletic training or participating in his other high school and community-service activities, Preston enjoys hanging out with his friends and family, playing video games, traveling, and watching sports.

Dr. Rocky D. Bilhartz is a physician and owner of HUSTLE3 (H3), a sports performance training facility in College Station, Texas, that uses technology and analytics to drive excellence in human performance. He has been the head coach of numerous teams in various sports at all youth levels, including the manager of multiple select/travel baseball teams from 2019-2024. Originally from Huntsville, Texas, Dr. Bilhartz holds an undergraduate degree from Rice University, and he earned his medical degree and MBA from Texas Tech University. He's a practicing interventional cardiologist and resides in the Bryan/College Station area with his wife, Lindsey, and their two sons, Preston and Peyton. Outside of his ongoing professional endeavors, he enjoys spending quality time with his family and strives to embody his own adage: *"Success always favors the one hustling."*

Index

A

Accessory Exercises 93, 96-98, 102, 104, 106, 108, 112
  Overhead Triceps Extension 97, 98, 104, 105, 108, 109, 112, 113
  Reverse Wrist Curl 96, 98, 104, 105, 108, 109, 112, 113
  Triceps Extension 97, 98, 104, 105, 108, 109, 112, 113
  Wrist Curl 96, 98, 104, 105, 108, 109, 112, 113
after the season 66
Ancore Pro 43, 97
arm band exercises. See also *arm bands*
  Back Rows 50, 103, 104, 107, 108, 111, 112
  Elevated External Rotation 48, 103, 104, 107, 108, 111, 112
  Elevated Internal Rotation 48, 103, 104, 107, 108, 111, 112
  External Rotation at Hip 49, 103, 104, 107, 108, 111, 112
  Forward Flies 48, 103, 104, 107, 108, 111, 112
  Internal Rotation at Hip 49, 103, 104, 107, 108, 111, 112
  Reverse Flies 49, 103, 104, 107, 108, 111, 112
  Standing "Y" 50, 103, 104, 107, 108, 111, 112
arm bands 37, 48-50, 62, 63, 65, 98, 103-105, 107-109, 111-113
Arm Care & Velo Program 37, 39, 40, 42, 45, 46, 62-66, 75, 76, 99, 101, 102, 105, 106, 109, 110, 113, 114
Arm Care & Velo Program Exercises
  arm bands 48-50, 62, 63, 65, 98, 103-105, 107-109, 111-113
  Cloud Touches 19, 46, 59, 103, 107
  cooldown 60-65, 103, 105, 107, 109-111, 113
    Bent-Over-Rows 60, 62, 63, 65, 103, 105, 107, 109, 111, 113
    Elevated Arm Hold 61-63, 65, 103, 105, 107, 109, 111, 113
    Horizontal Ball Hold 61-63, 65, 103, 105, 107, 109, 111, 113
    Kneeling Ball Hold 61-63, 65, 103, 105, 107, 109, 111, 113
    Presses 60, 62, 63, 65, 103, 105, 107, 109, 111, 113
    Rotational Presses 60, 62, 63, 65, 103, 105, 107, 109, 111, 113
    wrist weights & heavy plyo ball 60-63, 65, 103, 105, 109, 107, 111, 113
  Core Velocity Belt 40, 54-57, 103, 105, 107, 109
  Dynamic Warm-up Routine (abbreviated) 51
  myofascial release 47, 103-105, 107-109, 112, 113
  plyo ball throws
    Hip Finishers 54, 55, 57, 103, 105, 107, 109
    Reverse Throws 52, 103, 105, 107, 109
    Twist and Throws 53, 103, 105, 107, 109
    Weigh Mores 56, 57, 62, 103, 105, 107, 109
    Whip Behinds 19, 46, 58, 103, 107
Arm Circles & Flaps 11, 115
Arm Slot Drill Type 1 31, 32
Arm Slot Drill Type 2 31, 33

B

Balance Drill 24, 115
Ball Pick-Ups 86, 91, 115
baseball bag equipment 65
Bench Press 98, 102, 104-106, 108-110, 112, 113
Bent-Over Rows 60, 62, 63, 65, 103, 105, 107, 109, 111, 113
Blended Drill 31
bodyweight (strength) training 22, 86, 91, 92, 114, 115
Bottom Kickers 8, 51, 103, 104, 107, 108, 112, 115
Bulgarian Split Squats 86, 89, 91, 115
bullpen 40, 41, 62, 63, 69, 70, 75, 76, 78, 79, 99, 102, 103, 106, 107, 109-111, 113
  pitch count 75, 76, 78
Bullpen Pitching. See also *bullpen*

C

cards, as in *deck of playing cards* 91, 115
changeup 70, 72, 77, 79, 81
Chest Over Knee Drill 28, 115
Cloud Touches 19, 46, 59, 62, 103, 107
cooldown exercises
  Bent-Over-Rows 60, 62, 63, 65, 103, 105, 107, 109, 111, 113
  Elevated Arm Hold 61-63, 65, 103, 105, 107, 109, 111, 113
  Horizontal Ball Hold 61-63, 65, 103, 105, 107, 109, 111, 113

INDEX

Kneeling Ball Hold 61-63, 65, 103, 105, 107, 109, 111, 113
Presses 60, 62-63, 65, 103, 105, 107, 109, 111, 113
Rotational Presses 60, 62-63, 65, 103, 105, 107, 109, 111, 113
Core Velocity Belt 40, 54-57, 103, 105, 107, 109
Cradle Walks 9, 51, 103, 104, 107, 108, 112, 115
curveball 15, 70, 73, 74, 77, 79-81
   ideal age for 79

D

drills. See also *Learning to Pitch Drills*, *Learning to Throw Drills*, and *Arm Care & Velo Program Exercises*
Dynamic Warm-Up 8-11, 23, 51, 103-105, 107-109, 112, 113, 115. See also *Dynamic Warm-up Exercises*
Dynamic Warm-up Exercises
  Arm Circles & Flaps 11, 115
  Bottom Kickers 8, 51, 103, 104, 107, 108, 112, 115
  Cradle Walks 9, 51, 103, 104, 107, 108, 112, 115
  High Knees 8, 51, 103, 104, 107, 108, 112, 115
  Knee Huggers 9, 51, 103, 104, 107, 108, 112, 115
  Lunges with Twist 9, 51, 103, 104, 107, 108, 112, 115
  Shoulder Lifts 11, 115
  Side Lunges 10, 51, 103, 104, 107, 108, 112, 115

E

Elevated Arm Hold 61-63, 65, 103, 105, 107, 109, 111, 113
Equipment
  arm bands 37, 48-50, 62, 63, 65, 98, 103-105, 107-109, 111-113
  "Blue" Exercise Balance Pad 38, 52, 61
  Core Velocity Belt 40, 54-57, 103, 105, 107, 109
  foam roller 38
  Handheld Percussive Device 42
  home gym equipment 43, 95
  Marc Pro 42, 67
  Pitcher's Pocket Pro 9 Hole Net 41
  plyo balls 37, 52-57, 65, 103, 105, 107, 109, 111, 113
  plyo wall 39, 52-57
  Portolite Pitching Mound 40
  Radar with Display 42, 58, 59
  Rapsodo with Insight camera 43
  sock net 39, 58, 59
  TAP Bell Club 32, 33, 41
  TAP Connection Ball 32, 33, 41
  TAP Portable Plyo Mat 39
  TAP Training Sock 40, 65
  wrapped towel 30, 31, 38, 115
  wrist weights 37, 60, 62, 63, 65, 103, 107, 111
exercise balance pad 38, 52, 61

F

fastball 15, 69, 70-74, 76, 77, 79, 81, 103, 105, 107, 109, 111, 113
Flat-Ground Pitching 62, 64, 70, 75, 76, 102, 103, 105
foam roller 38
4-Step Windup 24, 115
functional training 83

G

Glove-Side Tuck Drill 29, 115
grip 70-74
  changeup 72
    2-Seam 72
    4-Seam 72
    Buddy Fingers 72
    Circle 72
  curveball 73
    Horseshoe 73
    Spike 73
    Standard 73
    Standard w/ Thumb High 73
  fastball 71
    2-Seam 71
    4-Seam 71
  slider 74
    4-Seam Offset 74
    Horseshoe 74
    Spike 74
    Standard High-Set 74
    Standard Low-Set 74
Grip and Elbow Flips 17
Groin Stretches 10, 51, 103, 104, 107, 108, 112, 115

H

handheld percussive device 42
High Knees 8, 51, 103, 104, 107, 108, 112, 115
high school 2, 3, 7, 14, 22, 37, 39, 43, 45, 66, 69, 70, 75, 76, 79, 83, 85, 93, 99, 101, 110, 119
Hop-Hop Throws 18
Horizontal Ball Hold 61-63, 65, 103, 105, 107, 109, 111, 113
HUSTLE3 2, 117, 119

I

in-season 3, 23, 46, 64, 65, 67, 75, 76, 99, 101, 106, 110-115
Insight camera 43

J

jogging 84, 85, 105

K

Knee Huggers 9, 51, 103, 104, 107, 108, 112, 115
Kneeling Ball Hold 61-63, 65, 103, 105, 107, 109, 111, 113

INDEX

L

Learning to Pitch Drills
   Arm Slot Drill Type 1 31, 32
   Arm Slot Drill Type 2 31, 33
   Balance Drill 24, 115
   Blended Drill 31
   Chest Over Knee Drill 28, 115
   4-Step Windup 24, 115
   Glove-Side Tuck Drill 29, 115
   Nose Over Toes Drill 26, 115
   Separation Drill 25, 31, 115
   Tape Down the Mound Drill 27, 115
   Towel Extension Drill 30, 31, 115
Learning to Throw Drills
   Cloud Touches 19
   Grip and Elbow Flips 17
   Hop-Hop Throws 18
   Rockers 18
   Twist and Throws 17
   Whip Behinds 19
lifts. See also *The Lifts*
long toss 46
Lunges with Twist 9, 51, 103, 104, 107, 108, 112, 115

M

Marc Pro 42, 67
Motus mTHROW Sleeve 80
myofascial release 47, 103-105, 107-109, 112, 113

N

Nose Over Toes Drill 26, 115

O

off-season 3, 45, 46, 62, 63, 66, 67, 75, 91, 99, 106, 114
Overhead Triceps Extension 97, 98, 104, 105, 108, 109, 112, 113

P

Pitcher's Pocket Pro 9 Hole Net 41
pitch-type 70, 78
   changeup 70, 72, 77, 79, 80, 103, 105, 107, 109, 111, 113
   curveball 15, 70, 73, 74, 77, 79-81, 103, 105, 107, 109, 111, 113
   cutter 78, 79
   fastball 15, 69, 70-74, 76, 77, 79, 81, 103, 105, 107, 109, 111, 113
   slider 74, 78, 79
plyo balls 37, 52-57, 65, 103, 105, 107, 109, 111, 113
   5 ounce 37, 56, 57, 103, 105, 107
   4.4 pound (2000 g) 37, 61-63, 65, 103, 105, 107, 109, 111, 113
   14 ounce 37, 53, 103, 105, 107, 109
   7 ounce 37, 54, 55, 65, 103, 105, 107, 109
   32 ounce 37, 52, 103, 105, 107, 109
   21 ounce 37, 52, 53, 103, 105, 107, 109
plyo ball throws. See Arm Care & Velo Program Exercises
plyo wall 39, 52-57
Portolite pitching mound 40
pre-season 3, 46, 63, 75, 106
Press 98, 102, 104-106, 108-110, 112, 113
Presses (with wrist weights) 60, 62, 63, 65, 103, 105, 107, 109, 111, 113
Pull Across & Pull Behinds 11, 51, 115
Push-Ups 86, 91, 115

R

radar 42, 58, 59
Rapsodo 43
resistance training 92, 98
rest & recovery 67
   Marc Pro 42, 67
Reverse Wrist Curl 98, 104, 105, 108, 109, 112, 113
Rockers 18
Roll Out 47, 103-105, 107-109, 112, 113
Rotational Presses 60, 62, 63, 65, 103, 105, 107, 109, 111, 113

S

Separation Drill 25, 31, 115
Shoulder Lifts 11, 115
Side Lunges 10, 51, 103, 104, 107, 108, 112, 115
Single-Leg Glute Bridges 86, 91, 115
Sit-Ups 86, 91, 115
slider 74, 78, 79
sock net 39, 58, 59
Spiders 10
Squat 86, 91, 98, 102, 104-106, 108-110, 112, 113, 115. See also *Bulgarian Split Squats*
Static Stretching 8, 91, 98, 103, 104, 107, 108, 112, 115
Static Stretching Exercises
   Groin Stretches 10, 51, 103, 104, 107, 108, 112, 115
   Pull Across & Pull Behinds 11, 115
   Spiders 10
Statue of Liberty 50, 103, 104, 107, 108, 111, 112
strength 2, 3, 6, 7, 14, 21-24, 28, 37, 38, 40, 42, 43, 45, 62, 66, 67, 69, 75, 83-86, 91, 93, 98, 99, 102, 112, 114, 115
Strength Program 43, 62, 83, 101, 102, 105, 106, 109, 110, 112-115

T

TAP Bell Club 32, 33, 41
TAP Connection Ball 32, 33, 41
Tape Down the Mound Drill 27, 115
TAP Portable Plyo Mat 39
TAP Training Sock 40, 65

INDEX

team practice 65, 110, 113
templates. See also *workout templates*
The Lifts 93-95, 98, 102, 106
   Bench Press 94, 98, 102, 104-106, 108-110, 112, 113
   Press 94, 95, 98, 102, 104-106, 108-110, 112, 113
   Squat 94, 98, 102, 104-106, 108-110, 112, 113, 115.
      See also *Bulgarian Split Squats*
Throwing Mechanics 14
towel 30, 31, 38, 115
Towel Extension Drill 30, 31, 115
Triceps Extension 95, 97, 98, 104, 105, 108, 109, 112, 113
Twist and Throws 17, 53, 103, 105, 107, 109

U

ulnar collateral ligament 66, 80

W

Warm-Up 6, 8, 23, 51, 103-105, 107-109, 111-113, 115
warm-up exercises
   arm bands 48-50, 62, 63, 65, 98, 103-105, 107-109, 111-113
     Back Rows 50, 103, 104, 107, 108, 111, 112
     Elevated External Rotation 48, 103, 104, 107, 108, 111, 112
     Elevated Internal Rotation 48, 103, 104, 107, 108, 111, 112
     External Rotation at Hip 49, 103, 104, 107, 108, 111, 112
     Forward Flies 48, 103, 104, 107, 108, 111, 112
     Internal Rotation at Hip 49, 103, 104, 107, 108, 111, 112
     Reverse Flies 49, 103, 104, 107, 108, 111, 112
     Standing "Y" 50, 103, 104, 107, 108, 111, 112
     Statue of Liberty 50, 103, 104, 107, 108, 111, 112
   Arm Circles & Flaps 11, 115
   Bottom Kickers 8, 51, 103, 104, 107, 108, 112, 115
   Cradle Walks 9, 51, 103, 104, 107, 108, 112, 115
   Groin Stretches 10, 51, 103, 104, 107, 108, 112, 115
   High Knees 8, 51, 103, 104, 107, 108, 112, 115
   Knee Huggers 9, 51, 103, 104, 107, 108, 112, 115
   Lunges with Twist 9, 51, 103, 104, 107, 108, 112, 115
   myofascial release 47, 103-105, 107-109, 112, 113
   Pull Across & Pull Behinds 11, 115
   Roll Out 47, 103-105, 107-109, 112, 113
   Shoulder Lifts 11, 115
   Side Lunges 10, 51, 103, 104, 107, 108, 112, 115
   Spiders 10
Weigh Mores 56, 57, 62, 103, 105, 107, 109
weightlifting. See also *The Lifts*
Whip Behinds 19, 46, 58, 103, 107
workout templates 101-115
Wrist Curl 98, 104, 105, 108, 109, 112, 113
wrist weights 37, 60-63, 65, 103, 107, 111

H3
TDB Field
"Hustle! Hustle! Hustle!"

www.ingramcontent.com/pod-product-compliance
Lightning Source LLC
Chambersburg PA
CBRC091725070526
44586CB00008B/82